BROADHEATH

1885 – 1985

A Century of Industry

by

FRANK BAMFORD

PHOTOGRAPHY

by

COLIN BAMFORD

First published in 1995 by
Frank Bamford, 9 Malvern Drive, Altrincham WA14 4NQ

ISBN 0 9517225 2 2

Typeset by Northern Writers Advisory Services, 77 Marford Crescent, Sale, Cheshire M33 4DN

Printed by Birkenhead Press, 1 & 3 Grove Road, Rock Ferry, Birkenhead, Merseyside L42 3XS

CONTENTS

LIST OF ILLUSTRATIONS

The figures were originally published in *Trade for the People.*

Chapter X

Chapter XII

INTRODUCTION

BROADHEATH is the story of the century, the hundred years from 1885 to 1985. During the first eighty years a great industrial estate slowly developed. In another twenty years it was virtually destroyed. This is surely a story which needs to be told in its own right, told before so many personal memories are lost.

Yet Broadheath is not an isolated area, nor its story an isolated tragedy. In the first place, it has been a vital and major part of the social and economic history of Altrincham and district since the industrial revolution of the last century which I related in *The Making of Altrincham 1850 – 1991* published a few years ago.

Altrincham passed through several phases in 150 years – market town, special satellite of Manchester supplying goods and services and especially high class homes, then the setting for industry which carried it deep into the twentieth century. Finally it has become a town of many parts, struggling to define an identity and a modern attractive physical shape.

The unique story of the great houses built in the mid-Victorian period on the south-west fringe of Altrincham was told in my book *Mansions and Men of Dunham Massey*. With the completion of the mansions in the early 1880s, this vibrant source of economic energy for the old market town had stabilised, but very soon a new dynamic force arose in the north-west, the great industrial area around the Bridgewater Canal, itself a major economic stimulus from a century earlier and still most important in the twentieth century. Such is the fascinating confluence of history.

Further, although the new industrial estate was the immediate result of local economic and geographical factors, in order for it to be properly understood it needs to be viewed in an even wider context. Its story derives essentially from the economic development of Britain in the nineteenth and twentieth centuries which I tried to explain in my first book *Trade for the People*.

So, in writing this new book on Broadheath, I have drawn on all my three previous volumes, particularly *Trade for the People*, in relating local to national economic developments and in relating Broadheath to Altrincham. In the local history context the book completes a trilogy with *Mansions and Men of Dunham Massey* and *The Making of Altrincham*.

In the four years since those books were written I have been very conscious of the fact that the Broadheath story was waiting to be told. Many local people have seemed to fall into two groups. One group is sublimely unaware of the importance of so recent a great industrial phenomenon on their doorsteps – or perhaps it was a happening they have preferred to treat as foreign to their own lives, an attitude typical of the general British intellectual and social attitude to making things, especially when, in the end, it seemed to be rather messy. The other group has consisted of the thousands of people who have worked, or are still working on the estate. Among the latter there has been a general fondness, nostalgia even for many, for the companies for which they have worked, as well as sadness for their decline or demise.

Of course, by no means everyone is in one of these two groups. There are also the 'don't knows' – those who have come to the area so recently or been too busy to know about Broadheath, knowing only the disreputable looking Atlantic Street they have passed on the main road or visited briefly to patronise one of the retail warehouses on once famous industrial sites.

I hope that all of these – particularly the don't knows, and the don't want to knows and even those who have known and loved, will find some enlightenment about Broadheath and Altrincham in this book. I hope, too, that all of them will have a fresh appreciation of the interesting and vital science and business of making things.

The 'century' begins in 1885, the first year of operation of George Richards and Company, and ends in 1985 by which time, as will appear, Broadheath had changed almost beyond recognition. Although I have briefly brought the stories of some companies more up-to-date and tried to give a general impression of the area in 1995, I have not sought to provide a detailed account of the last ten years.

I

THE BRITISH ECONOMY IN THE LATE NINETEENTH CENTURY

The half century which ended in 1880 was the most frenetic and significant period of economic expansion ever experienced, not only in Britain but indeed in the world. Whilst the shoots of the Industrial Revolution, essentially in the textile businesses, were already strong by 1830, their dramatic flowering followed in the next fifty years with rapid and almost continuous expansion. The consumption of cotton yarn in Britain, mainly from the southern USA, rose from 250,000 lbs in the 1830s to 1,100,000 lbs in 1870. Exports of cotton piece goods rose from 600 million yards in 1830 to 4000 million yards in 1880. Total exporrts grew from 10% of gross national product in 1831 to 25% in 1871.

Britain, as leader in technology and trade, dominated the world business in textiles in this era. The cotton manufacturers, almost all in family businesses, became immensely wealthy from the profits made in Manchester and south Lancashire, as, to a lesser extent, did woollen manufacturers in Yorkshire. Enormous amounts of capital became available for other enterprises, most notably railway investment at home and abroad. Net foreign investment grew from around £5 million per annum in the 1830s to around £75 million per annum in the 1870s. Between 1830 and 1860 the principal country-wide network of railways, which endured for more than a hundred years, was constructed at a cost of some £600 millions or well over £20 billion in 1990s' money.

A vital spin-off from all this great burst of industrial activity was the emergence of a dynamic financial system not only in the banking field but also, crucially, in the invention of the joint stock company with limited liability, which came to be the essential engine of the modern capitalist system. It was not the textile industry which directly invoked this financial invention, since that business was mainly self-financing, but rather the building of the railways, the first major investment programme in the world to mobilise the spare capital and savings of a wide range of people.

There were of course major industrial consequences of the explosion of economic activity in textiles and the railways, most importantly in the iron and steel industries and engineering, with shipbuilding an im-

1. Figure: Exports of Cotton Textiles Quantities and Prices 1820-1880.

EXPORT OF COTTON PIECE GOODS

	(million yards)		(million yards)
1820	300	1870	2700
1830	600	1880	4000
1840	1100	1890	5000
1850	1600	1900	5200
1860	2000		

A. Exports of cotton piece goods (million yards) (lefthand scale)

B. Index of export prices for cotton textiles (righthand scale, 1820=100)

Note: This is a simplified picture showing approximate positions reached at discrete points in time. It conceals large temporary fluctations cause by variations in trade.

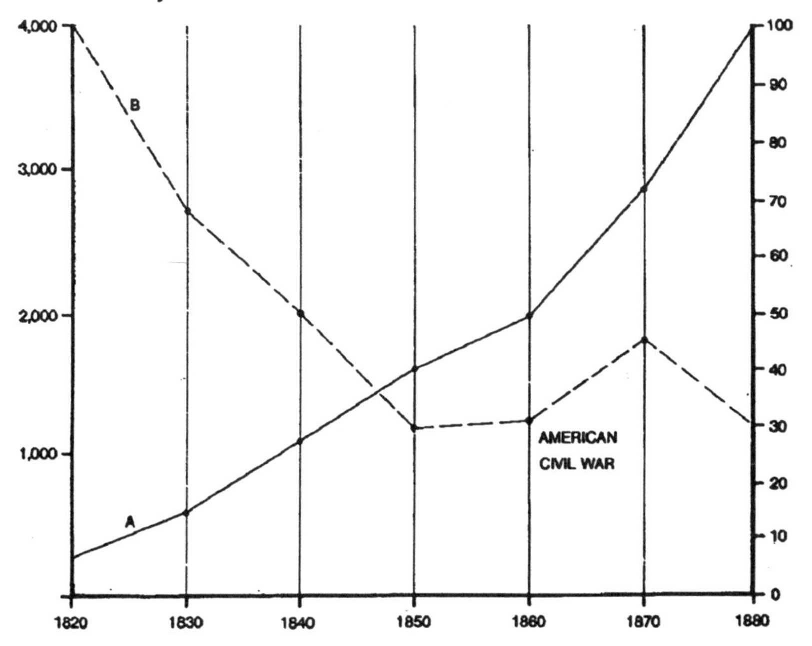

portant beneficiary of the vast increase in international trade.

The supply of labour for the great expansion of industry and commerce came partly from a steady increase in total population but it was particularly associated with the release of workers from agriculture resulting from the enclosure movement, as well as increases in productivity and the growing import of food from abroad. The concentration of people in workshops and factories was inevitably associated with the mushrooming creation of towns and cities. Manchester, at the heart of it all, more than quadrupled from 70,000 to 300,000 people in the first half of the nineteenth century, increasing further to 500,000 and more by 1880. The intensive building of tiny back-to-back houses took place at a time when the need for decent sanitation and even clean water was barely appreciated. Thus even towards the end of the century vast numbers of people in Manchester and elsewhere lived in appalling conditions of factory noise, smells and smoke as well as of poor sanitation and endemic disease and lack of social amenities and welfare.

By 1880, however, much was beginning to change. Looking back from the perspective of the late twentieth century it is hardly surprising that the frenetic pace of economic development in the middle fifty years of the nineteenth century could not be maintained. This extraordinary pace had resulted from the unique coincidence of the technological developments in textiles, power and railways which had given

2. Figure: Steel Production 1870-1913: USA, Germany and UK.

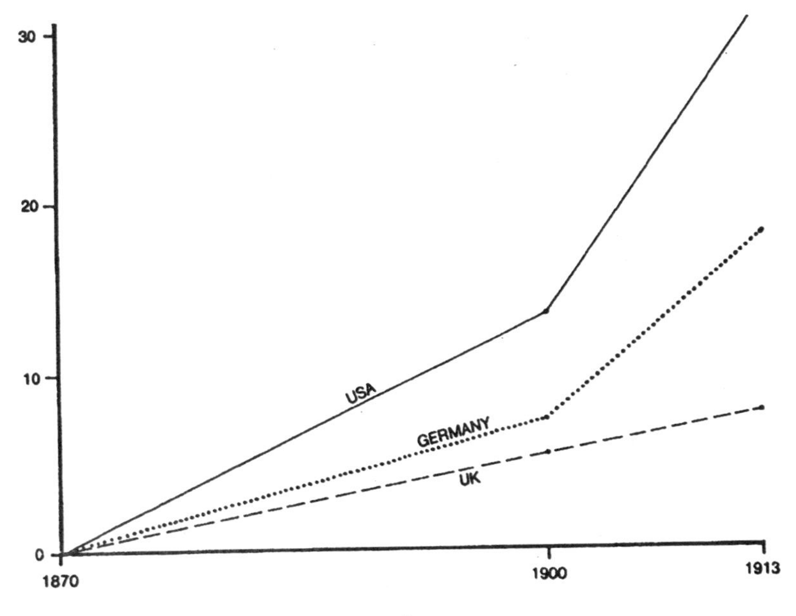

British capitalists a temporary near-monopoly in world trade and the opening up of the continents.

As the century drew towards its close and the railway boom, even overseas, slowed down, other countries in Europe, particularly Germany, and North America, were beginning to compete in the textile and related businesses and were developing their newer industries behind tariff and other barriers. Export trade became more competitive and difficult while opportunities for vastly profitable overseas investments began to dwindle, so there was more money for investment at home.

The opening up of continents resulted in greatly improved supplies of food at much reduced prices. Cereals cost only half as much in the 1880s as in the 1860s, and even meat prices fell by a quarter. A more varied supply of food came from many countries. Real wages appear to have increased about 50% in twenty five years in the last part of the century. With improving regulation of factories and mines, there was a significant amelioration of working and living conditions. The late nineteenth century witnessed the real beginnings of a tolerable existence for the large urban working class. The so-called Great Depression brought great benefits for those with jobs, though unemployment was increasingly recognised as a serious problem. There remained, moreover, enormous social and economic inequality with huge profits in private hands, much of which continued to be invested abroad.

Another vital aspect of the British condition was that so much of the country's capital, managerial and just plain human resources, were tied up in the original basic industries, so the country was ill-equipped to meet the challenges of other European countries, as well as the USA, which had come in on the second, protected, wind of industrialisation and therefore had more than a head's start in the newer businesses of the twentieth century. The British industrialists, who led the world in textiles in the nineteenth century, proved unable to maintain their leadership by transferring adequate resources to the production of more capital intensive commodities or those incorporating a high degree of productive skill or expertise. They allowed other countries to take the lead.

Before long, it became clear that the British class system which developed in the nineteenth century was singularly ill-designed to assume the economic burdens of the twentieth century. The lack of industrial professionalism among the moneyed classes has become a legend, no less true for that. These classes did, however, make one great discovery – the public school, with its basically classical education. For the working classes, education was grudgingly doled out. Technical and vocational education was sadly neglected, compared with Germany. There a strong state school system with a substantial technical content was established in the nineteenth century, meanwhile Britain was still dependent largely on a voluntary system of basic education.

There are many indications of the extent to which Britain fell behind in the newer and more sophisticated world economy. Iron and steel exports actually fell during the 1880s. UK output of pig-iron fell from 46% of the world total in the late 1870s to 14% in 1914. In the newer engineering industries right through to the even newer motor vehicles as well as in chemicals, British industry was generally left behind, stranded in its conservative commitment to old lines of business and old ways of doing things.

At no stage was there an adequate capability in depth in Britain, either in management or highly educated and trained manpower at the professional or craftsman level, to compete effectively over a wide industrial field in all the newer industries. The plain fact was that the industries in which Britain had led the world and in which she still held an advantage, i.e. mainly textiles, coal and even iron and steel, depended on the availability of substantial capital investment but more particularly of cheap low-grade labour which was obedient and compliant. The newer and more sophisticated industries required more highly skilled and educated operatives capable of taking more independent action. The British failure to provide both reasonable general education for the working people, and more specifically technical and vocational education, was entirely consistent with the failure of industrialists to perceive the longer term opportunities and needs. In this respect they were very different from the Americans and especially the Germans.

It was around the turn of the century that the working classes began to organise themselves in trade unions and to seek separate political representation. We do not have the space in this book to develop this aspect of British economic history, but it is very relevant as background to the Broadheath story that there have always been two 'sides' in industry – the bosses and the workers, reflecting the social class system. As we shall see, one important local company sought to bridge the gap to some extent.

It was perhaps the fact of the early advanced position of British industry in the mid-nineteenth century which before long led to manufacturing industry becoming unfashionable among the upper classes and the intelligentsia. The public schools, to which so many of the newly-rich industrialists sent their sons, were more attuned to the professions, the church and the civil and colonial services (for this after all was the great period of Empire) than to making things. In so far as the intelligentsia were attracted at all to the world of business, they generally preferred the remunerative commercial and financial operations centred on the City of London. Britain's pre-eminence in international trade and shipping and in lending money led to a fast-growing business in financial services which stood on its own feet as a substantial contribution to the national wealth. So it was understandable and arguably justifiable that bright young men should be attracted to it.

There were, however, some serious consequences. First, the drain on the limited supply of educated people, who in any event were not technically educated, was such that even fewer such people were available for the more down-to-earth business of making things rather than money. Secondly, the banking and financial businesses developed so profitably and so independently and internationally, that they became increasing detached from industry. Thus the provision of finance for manufacturing investment in the UK, particularly long-term finance, was never a major activity for the banking community in the same way as it was in other countries and particularly in Germany.

These substantial handicaps to British industrial progress in the twentieth century should not, however, be taken to mean that manufacturing was generally unsuccessful or insignificant. Even in the last fifteen years before 1914 exports rose by over 50%, but the Germans were now buying British coal rather than manufactured goods, on which they were levying a 25% tariff. Industry continued to be of essential importance to the economy with many important enterprises being profitable over long periods. But compared to its counterparts in some other countries, it has been always significantly handicapped and so more prone to damaging set-backs as international competition has become more intense and world financial movements more severe. It is also commonplace to report that the British have always been very inventive but poorly organised to exploit new inventions with effective commercial effort and industrial investment. It will be interesting to see how far Broadheath has reflected these general business characteristics.

II
MANCHESTER AND ALTRINCHAM

We have already noted that the population of Manchester grew from 70,000 in 1800 to over 500,000 by 1880 – much more if one counts the outer suburbs. Throughout this period the city was always the production centre of the cotton industry which spread westwards from the Pennines across south Lancashire, much of it concentrating in larger factories in and around Manchester as steam power freed it from dependence on running water. Although originally very important in cotton spinning, Manchester tended to move later towards the finishing trades, including calico printing. It also progressively became the great commercial and financial centre of the industry.

The unprecedented and unparalleled industrial development concentrated in the cotton metropolis resulted, as we have noted, in appalling living and working conditions. The factories themselves produced not only vast quantities of textiles but also great nuisances of dirt, effluent, smoke and noise and therefore disease. From around the middle of the century, the public health movement resulted in considerable effort to improve these conditions but progress was slow – almost Canute-like in its efforts against the tides of more and bigger factories and increased population. Even in 1894, Robert Blatchford in his *Merrie England* railed against hypocritical Manchester factory owners who forced their workers to live in slums, lacking "pure air, bright skies, clean rivers, clean streets and beautiful fields", but who themselves retreated to suburbs "as far from the factories as they can get".

In the latter part of the nineteenth century, the demand for land for commercial purposes in the city centre and increasing specialisation in the textile business were tending to move some of the cotton factory production away from the city into other towns. At the same time the Manchester area was beginning to experience the effects of economic diversification. Clearly the textile and railway industries greatly stimulated other industries, initially to meet their own requirements for engines and machinery as well as for specialised materials including chemicals.

As regards the latter, manufacturers of soaps, dyes and inks expanded both their scientific knowledge and their sales to other markets. A number of Manchester firms were highly successful in marketing coal-tar dyes. The use of waste from local gasworks stimulated the production of sulphocyanides, carbolic acid was produced from coal-tar and a number of profitable soda factories appeared. Knowledge gained from these activities also stimulated expansions in rubber-making and the brewing industry.

Similarly, engineering took on an economic life of its own. Manchester and its regions became important in the manufacture of steam engines, railway locomotives, machine tools and armaments. Textile machinery was supplied to the expanding textile industries in other countries. (The term 'machine tools' is used in this book to denote equipment supplied to manufacturers to make products of various kinds. Most importantly in Broadheath, these tools include boring and grinding machines.)

Well before these industrial and engineering developments, the rapid growth of Manchester had depended on the solution to the problems of the supply of materials, food and fuel. Most notably, raw cotton had to come mainly from the southern USA and had therefore depended on the importation there of slaves from Africa. There was dependence, too, on the port of Liverpool, resentment about which led, somewhat belatedly, to the construction of the Manchester Ship Canal by 1894. By greatly facilitating the carriage of heavy freight, the canal made it possible for Manchester to become a great centre of engineering.

Well over a century earlier another canal had begun to play a vital role in the development of the city. In 1761 the Duke of Bridgewater opened his canal to bring coal from his mines at Worsley into Manchester. Originally important for heating buildings, coal became the fuel for steam power which drove textile machinery for most of the nineteenth century.

This great canal was soon found to have other vital uses, particularly for bringing food to Manchester multitudes. It was soon extended south and west from the city into Cheshire's fertile fields, reaching Broadheath by 1775 and thence to the Mersey estuary at Runcorn. It appears that a major cargo comprised vegetables and other farm produce from the Altrincham area loaded at the Duke's warehouse and transported on barges into the city. On the return journey a barge would typically be loaded with human manure from the privies of Manchester to fertilise the fields so that they could produce even more food...

Undoubtedly the supply of food for the cotton metropolis was of major economic importance to the Altrincham area in the first half of the nineteenth century, when the population of the old market town grew from around 1,700 to almost 4,500 by 1851. Some of this increase must of course be attributed to the increasing tendency for professional men and industrialists to commute from the Altrincham area to Manchester even before the railway was opened in 1849. The most notable of these was William Neild, a leading member of a Manchester calico printing firm who travelled daily from his house, High Lawn, built in Bowdon in the 1840s. Many other men commuted by canal from Broadheath, notably on the express or 'flyer' barges which did the journey within a hour, although the well-to-do would ride in their coaches.

If the rate of growth of Altrincham had been rapid in the first half of the century, it became quite phenomenal thereafter. In thirty years the population grew from around 4,500 to 11,250. In mid-century it was a scattered township in three main and separated areas – Higher Town around the Market Place, Lower Town around George Street and the south-western areas from Regent Road to the Downs and the beginning of Lloyd Street, with fields in between and close by. By 1880 Altrincham was thoroughly built up and consolidated from Barrington Road and Derby Street in the north to Hale Road in the south, bounded by the railway on the east and increasingly by middle and upper class houses in the west, towards Dunham Road.

Of course a continuing high growth rate was to be expected as the demand for supplies and services, including commuting services to Manchester, increased as that city expanded. But the spectacular nature of the town's growth must be associated particularly with the unique creation of a wealthy estate of great houses and mansions around the new church of St Margaret's, completed in 1855 as the parish church of Dunham Massey. (The full story of this astonishing development is told in the writer's book *Mansions and Men of Dunham Massey.*)

The men of Dunham Massey, the owners of the mansions, were mainly cotton manufacturers with factories in Manchester (and a few in Stockport) who had chosen to live in the delectable south-western countryside within commuting distance of the works. There were among them also professional people and business men, earning comfortable livings from working for the cotton barons, and including surgeons, architects, solicitors, bankers and, notably, wine and spirit mer-

Map of Altrincham (from O.S. map) This map was published in 1882 and shows how well the town was developed from Sandiway and Derby Street in the north to the Devisdale and Hale Road in the south. Many of the Mansions of Dunham Massey can be seen in the south-west, as well as the large houses of Bowdon. The new hospital can be seen on the corner of Bowdon Road (now Market Street) and Chapel Road (now Regent Road). However, the new 'Altrincham and Bowdon Station' which was opened in 1881 near 'Altrincham Junction' does not appear, nor does Stamford New Road.

chants. Potentially relevant to our present study, rather late arrivals in Dunham Massey were William and Francis Crossley who built up their engineering business with a great works at Openshaw which later became Crossley Motors.

By 1880 it appears that the total income of the men of Dunham Massey was something like twice the total of all incomes of the rest of the inhabitants of Altrincham. The building of the mansions, and their subsequent servicing and supplying, undoubtedly provided a great stimulus to the economy of the whole area in the mid-Victorian period. It is perhaps significant that following the completion of the building of the mansions the rate of increase in the population of the town slowed markedly – only 1,175 more people in the 1880s compared with 2,771 in the 1870s on the heels of the biggest spurt in mansion building.

So, by 1880, Altrincham was a fully developed town with a new railway station, hospital, market hall and a solid phalanx of dwellings of all sizes from streets of tiny houses, later to be condemned as slums, through swathes of middle class villas to the most extravagant mansions. Here was a town ready and waiting for further economic stimulation which came from industry, of which it had virtually no previous experience except from a few textile workshops.

III
INDUSTRY COMES TO BROADHEATH

Just over half a mile north of the town centre the main road to Sale and Manchester was crossed by the Bridgewater Canal with the wharf and the Duke's warehouse close by. Barely 100 yards further north was the Warrington and Stockport Railway and 500 yards further the line from West Timperley to Glazebrook and Liverpool, and between them lay the hamlet of Broadheath around the main road. To the east some 600-700 yards away ran the line from Altrincham to Manchester. Clearly the area around the canal/road junction was in a wonderful position for industrial development. Communications and transport potential seemed excellent in all directions. Close by was the newly developed town of Altrincham. Between the town and Broadheath was a considerable area of farm land which could conceivably be used for housing although the fashionable area for expansion was at the other end of the town.

All that was required was land which could be used for industry. One could well understand the incentive for industrialists not only to live in this attractive area, but also to bring their factories there so that good quality workers could be recruited to live in pleasant surroundings, and they themselves could pleasantly and conveniently live near their factories. On the other hand, so many industrialists had moved to the area already in order to escape from the industrial gloom of Manchester, it is easy to imagine that they would not exactly welcome the arrival of factories on their doorsteps. This point was undoubtedly in the mind of Lord Stamford, the original owner of most of the land in the Altrincham area, who controlled its use through restrictive covenants. His policy was apparently to prevent industrial use of any land to the south of the canal, so banishing industry nearly a mile from the mansions and half a mile from the main part of the town.

Consistent with this policy the first factory opened in 1885. Significantly it was introduced by an American engineer, George Richards, who established his Atlantic Engineering Works, in 4½ acres just off the main road to Sale between the canal and the first railway bridge, thus giving the name Atlantic Street to the road which eventually reached westwards for nearly a mile. It was in fact a clear case of a

4. An early boring and turning mill made by George Richards and Company (1912). (Reproduced from The Engineer, 1912.)

move from Manchester where George Richards had first established his Atlantic Works. George Richards arrived in Europe as a young engineer in 1877 and travelled to Sweden where for a time he was associated with Kopings, the manufacturers of wood-working machinery. In 1880 he came to England and teamed up with a Mr Atkinson and opened a works in City Road, Manchester, making woodworking machinery. The business expanded and moved into machine tools, particularly horizontal boring machines, in a factory at Broadheath.

When George Richards came to Broadheath there was no inkling of the prospect of the development of a major industrial estate in the area. In fact nothing more happened until the mid-1890s when there was a flurry of companies moving from Manchester – Thornton-Pickard, makers of photographic apparatus, Luke and Spencer, makers of abrasive products and grinding machines, both in Atlantic Street, H F O'Brien and Company, oil merchants, with a depot in Brunswick Street across the main road, and finally the all-important Tilghmans.

J E Thornton was a photographic inventor from Manchester who had by 1887 registered twelve patents, mainly for camera shutters. As an apprentice he had already designed a camera and a roller blind shutter. By 1885 he had established a small manufacturing unit and an office near Deansgate. His operations seem to have been more or less continuously in some kind of financial crisis which led him into partnership with the Pickard family, businessmen with money but no photographic experience. In 1888 the Thornton Manufacturing Company, making cameras, was renamed Thornton-Pickard which in 1891 decided to move to a purpose-built factory at Broadheath. Both Thornton and Edgar Pickard made their homes in Altrincham. They quarrelled interminably about the conduct of the business.

Because of the financial situation of the company, Thornton had to concede control to the Pickards. In 1897 it was turned into a public limited company. An attempt was made to enter the US market through Boston, but it did not prosper. In Europe no proper patent protection had been secured and German companies copied the Thornton-Pickard shutters without redress. A serious fall in profits in 1897 caused Thornton to complain that the company was not keeping

5. The Thornton-Pickard works on Atlantic Street. (From company brochure, pre-1914.)

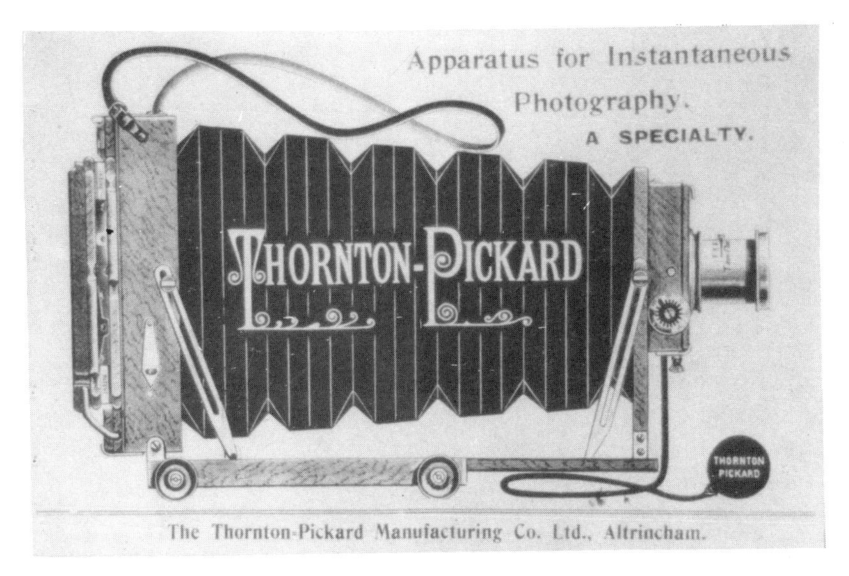

6. The Thornton-Pickard 'Ruby' camera. (From a company brochure, pre-1914.)

up with its competitors, being managed by people who did not understand the business. He left the company and started his own photographic supply company; the building it occupied is still standing in Oakfield Road, Altrincham. Thornton-Pickards prospered tolerably well and its products were known world-wide. Its heyday was just before the First World War when it employed 250 people, but its profitability was improved by war-time orders and the development of the aerial camera. It did, however, go out of business in 1939, apparently as a result of poor investment and outdated production methods.

Luke and Spencer was another all-British company which was established in 1877 and was therefore one of the oldest firms in the country producing abrasive wheels. In that year, Robert Luke and Mountfield Spencer purchased the business of Slacks Emery Wheel Company in Ardwick, Manchester. Eighteen years later the new company transferred its activities to Broadheath.

The Tilghman brothers, 'B C and R A', came from Pennsylvania, USA. The story goes that in the 1860s General B C Tilghman was stationed in the American south-west where, after the Civil War, the army was hard pressed to keep raiding Apaches and Commanches in check. The windows of the army post were being continually affected by frequent sandstorms which soon obscured them unless they were

7. The Thornton-Pickard woodwork shop. (From company brochure, pre-1914.)

8. An early sand blast machine made by Tilghmans (1901). (From company brochure.)

9. A two-stage air compressor made by Tilghmans (1911). (From company brochure, pre-1914.)

protected by a wire frame. This experience led General Tilghman to design a machine which produced a blast of sand and air. This was originally used – with specially prepared stencils – for decorating glass.

However, it was soon realised that this process was ideal for cleaning metal castings and forgings, and it was quickly adopted by the metal trades. Later it was realised that sand was a danger to health and it was replaced by iron and steel shot.

The Tilghman brothers came over to England in the 1870s, set up their first sand-blast machinery factory in London and later moved to Sheffield. It appears that they were acquainted with George Richards at an early stage and provided finance for him at the time he moved his factory to Broadheath. B C Tilghman owned most of the Richards' shares and was chairman of the company in 1886, with George Richards as secretary and managing director. The accounts for 1885, the first year of operation, showed a balance of £786. The directors referred to the depression in all branches of business in the period. Richards appears not to have been a good manager and in 1891 resigned without notice. Up to that time, losses had exceeded profits and a stocktaking and inventory examination produced 'surprising' results. The board decided to follow "a less adventurous and speculative course". There were heavy losses in the next few years and in 1895 the directors were authorised to sell the business as a going concern.

In 1896 Tilghmans not only moved their own operations to Broadheath but also took over George Richards and Company. At first the two companies occupied premises on either side of Atlantic Street, roughly where MFI and Broadprint now stand. In 1902 they were formally merged. In 1910 Tilghmans began to build a large factory on the

10. Sir Joseph Lawrence, the first chairman and managing director of the Linotype and Machinery Company (From company brochure, pre-1914.)

north side of the railway line which was mainly occupied by Richards until the late 1960s.

In 1895 the Altrincham Electric Supply Company built a generating station in Broadheath to provide power for the factories and elsewhere, so that electric lamps began to appear barely half a century after gas had replaced oil. A private company was empowered to proceed with the project subject to a specific obligation to sell the undertaking to Altrincham Urban District Council if so requested at 7½% above the costs expended. In 1904 the council enquired what the purchase figure would be and was told £99,343. After hesitating for six months, the Council was unable to arrive at a definite decision and the company finally withdrew its offer in July 1905. Thirty years later the Sale Urban District Council bought that part of the undertaking supplying power to Ashton-upon-Mersey.

So the industrial estate was beginning to take shape, but its impact on the Altrincham area was very limited until there came about, in the last few years of the nineteenth century, an astonishing industrial initiative which really seemed to belong much later in the twentieth century. The Linotype and Machinery Company had been originally es-

11. The Linotype factory from the Bridgewater Canal. (From company brochure, pre-1914.)

tablished in Manchester by a group of quite eminent British people to exploit an American invention of a printing machine which enabled type to be set by the use of a keyboard similar to that of a typewriter. Using this machine a single operator could take the place of six people setting type by hand. Prominent among the founders of the British company were Sir Joseph Lawrence MP and one-time Sheriff of London and Lord Kelvin, a famous scientist.

In the late 1890s the company decided to develop a very large industrial operation at Broadheath for which they would need many hundreds of good workers, many of them skilled. In order to attract and retain such people, they wished to build a major housing estate with all associated amenities in the form of allotments and sports grounds. For this purpose they required some 40 acres of land within reasonable walking distance of Altrincham town centre with the houses close to the factory. There was only one site which met these criteria – south of the canal to the west of the main road from Altrincham to Sale. Of course the policy of the Earl of Stamford was opposed to industry south of the canal. Perhaps he was persuaded by the fact that only four acres next to the canal would be used for the factory with the rest devoted to housing and amenity purposes. Certainly the proposed development would leave very little room for other indus-

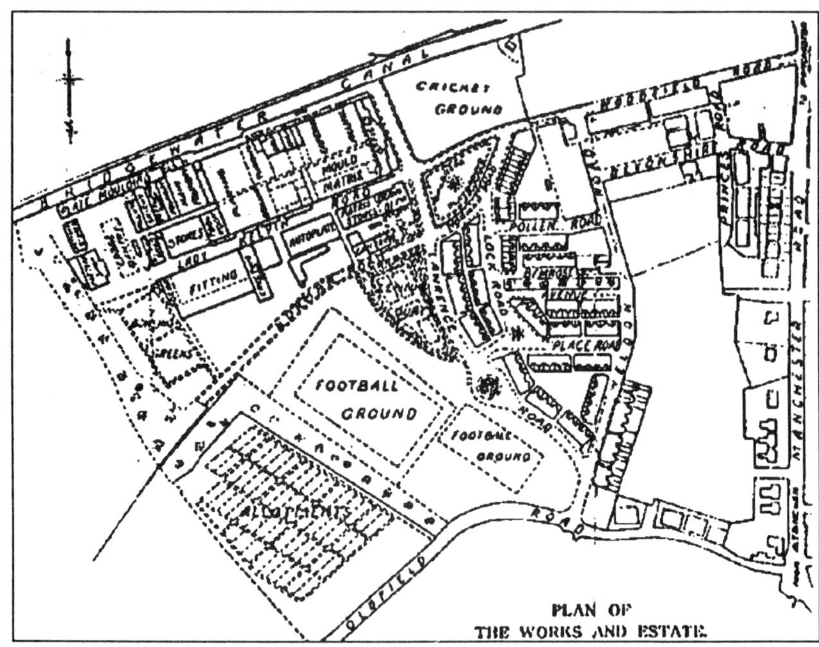

12. The original plans of the Linotype works and estate.

trial use south of the canal.

The Linotype Company built 172 five to seven-roomed houses for its employees which were let to them at half the rentals prevailing in the neighbourhood, together with recreation facilities, comprising two football grounds, a cricket ground, four tennis courts, two bowling greens and a playground for children, plus extensive allotments. The generosity of these provisions was a vivid and practical expression of a management philosophy which also involved the organisation of a works committee in which employee representatives could have a say in how the company was run, as well as a system of profit sharing, providing for employees to receive a substantial part of cost savings.

The Linotype estate, which seems to have mainly to the idea of Sir Joseph Lawrence MP, could have been partly inspired by Port Sunlight, built by Lord Leverhulme for his employees in the 1890s or by Bournville which was built by the Cadbury family around 1893. There was, in fact, an even earlier and quite unique example in the 1850s and 1860s when Sir Titus Salt, a wealthy woollen textile manufacturer, was so appalled at the living conditions in and around Bradford, which he judged were calculated to deprave and debauch, that he built a town, Saltaire, around his factory. In 1871 this housed over 4,000 people. There is a distinct similarity between the Linotype houses, with their black and white gables, and one large block of houses at Port Sunlight.

The Linotype housing estate was carefully and tastefully planned with trees and areas of grass. The houses were designed in pairs, some with shared gables and steeply pitched roofs.

Houses were graded in different streets according to the grading of the factory employees, the larger houses containing bathrooms. Each road was named after a director of the company. Without doubt, the quality of the houses was in general a cut above that of the existing working class streets in the town, or even of the other streets nearby which were also built in the last years of the last century, i.e. Princes Street and Woodfield and Devonshire Roads.

The fact that so much land was devoted to housing and social amenities should not obscure the fact that the Linotype factory itself was huge. The company boasted that its main 'workshop' was four times as big as Westminster Hall. Its operations were undoubtedly

13. Lawrence Road: the most elegant of the streets on the Linotype estate.

14. The Linotype Composing Machine. (From company brochure, pre-1914.)

most successful. Before the First World War, Linotype machines were used for printing most of the country's newspapers and the number of employees rose to 2,000 – and more in busy times.

Clearly this was an immense project requiring considerable finance. The original cost of the whole project was stated to be from £250,000 to £300,000 – of the order of £10 million in 1995 money. It is not surprising that the necessary funds for the initial cost and the development of the business did not come mainly from the British banking system which, as we have noted, has always been reluctant to invest in industry on a long-term basis. We do not know what efforts were made to secure backing finance but in fact the company turned to the American Mergenthaler Company from

15. The Miehle printing press made by Linotype. (From company brochure, pre-1914.)

16. The Sheffield Daily Telegraph installation of twenty-seven Linotype compositing machines. (From company brochure, pre-1914.)

which they had taken the Linotype licence. In return for money, the American company received shares – to the point that by 1909 it controlled the British company and sent its own representative to run it. We know that in 1921 both the chairman and managing director were American.

17. Navigation Road School – opened in 1906.

The American company had perceived the great potential in the imaginative project on which the British company had so confidently and successfully embarked. In retrospect it seems a pity that the project could not have remained British in finance and management, despite the fact that it was exploiting an American invention.

For the inauguration ceremony for the Broadheath plant in 1899, a special train brought eighty people from London. Lord Kelvin addressed some remarks to trade unionists, "They must do their allies and friends on the other side of the Atlantic the justice to perceive in them a degree of inventive genius and a practical way of bringing into use for the benefit of mankind on which they had scarcely yet entered into in the older country."

Clearly the arrival of Linotype as the seventh company, and much the largest so far, had put Broadheath firmly on the map as an industrial estate. Private house-building already been stimulated in the area and the population of Altrincham increased by the staggering total of 4,407 in the ten years to 1901, by far the largest expansion of all. Substantial commercial enterprises also appeared such as the building now occupied by Barclays Bank on the corner of Atlantic Street and Manchester Road, which bears the date 1900. Navigation Road School was built for 800 children by 1906 and the Broadheath Recreation Ground was established nearby. A new church, St Albans, was also built on the corner of Lindsell and Manchester Roads, in the early years of the century.

Although it is true that seven companies, which include the Electric

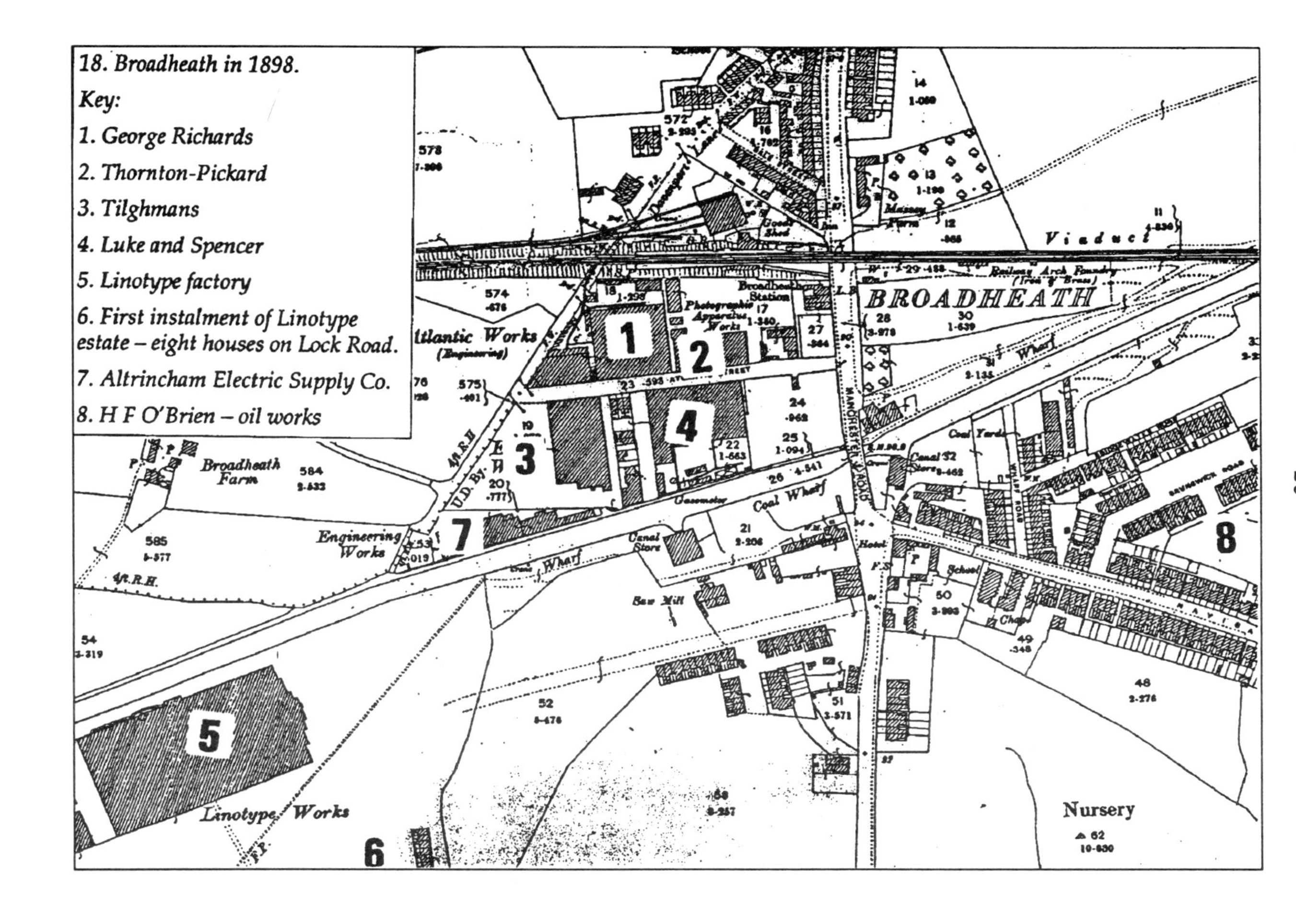

18. Broadheath in 1898.

Key:

1. George Richards
2. Thornton-Pickard
3. Tilghmans
4. Luke and Spencer
5. Linotype factory
6. First instalment of Linotype estate – eight houses on Lock Road.
7. Altrincham Electric Supply Co.
8. H F O'Brien – oil works

Supply Company, are not a large sample, it is perhaps instructive to consider their nature and origins. Of the four more technical companies three, Richards, Tilghmans and Linotype, all had strong American connections. All of them prospered, although Richards was apparently in trouble until it was taken over by Tilghmans. Thornton-Pickard was thoroughly British – very inventive but not very good in commercial exploitation. However, the other British company, Luke and Spencer, prospered and lasted for the better part of a century.

Into the Twentieth Century

By 1914 another seven companies had come to Broadheath.

Castleton Steam Packing (1904)
producing packing for engines. The company built a street of houses for its workers next to its factory on the south side of Atlantic Street.

Radium (Broadheath) Limited (1904)
producing a process for suede and leather dyes plus the manufacture of all kinds of leather dressings and finishes for the shoe trade.

In 1904 Mr Squire Lord moved his leather dressing firm from Eccles to an old iron foundry in Bridgewater Road. It was there that the Radium Company was formed to manufacture the well-known Radium leather and satin dyes, as well as all kinds of leather finishes and household polishes. Radium later began making their own tins for their products and were so successful in this that they decided to produce tins for the open market. This new business was organised in a separate company, Lord Bros. Ltd, working in the same factory.

Charles Madan & Co (1903)
makers of steam injectors in the Vortex Works on the canal side of Atlantic Street. The Vortex story began in a Salford backroom in 1889 when two young engineers, Charles S Madan and John MacKenzie, formed the company to manufacture pumping machinery for general marine and naval engineering. In 1903 they built a new works in Broadheath and took thirty men on their payroll. By this time they were also making pumping machines for many other branches of industry.

Leathers Company (Altrincham) Ltd.
who manufactured hydraulic leather packings. They had started in Stretford in 1888 and were the largest manufacturers of this type of

19. H W Kearns: early transport of machines. (Newspaper picture 1960, County Express.)

packing. They also had a works in Grafton Street in Altrincham.

H W Kearns (1907)
who were to become one of the world's leading machine tool makers.

Mr H W Kearns, a chemistry graduate of London University with experience in the making of baby food and in the dyeing industry, had had a major share-holding in the machine tool company of William Muirs with a factory in one of the poorest parts of Salford, a location which Kearns knew would never attract the best kind of labour or provide the ideal conditions for making accurate machinery. When the company declined to accept his proposal for moving the factory, he withdrew his investment of £30,000 and built his own factory at Broadheath, bringing twenty-eight men from Muirs. It was a private company and remained so for nearly half a century.

Kearns was friendly with Mathewson, the managing director of George Richards and Tilghmans. After both companies had flirted with an agreement with Frank Pearns, a Manchester manufacturer who had designed a modern machine centre, they continued to go their separate ways with Richards developing a wide variety of machine tools, including some bearing the Pearns name and especially the horizontal boring machine, in which they eventually specialised, whilst Kearns concentrated on a new type of universal horizontal boring, milling and drilling machine. There were clearly some quite close

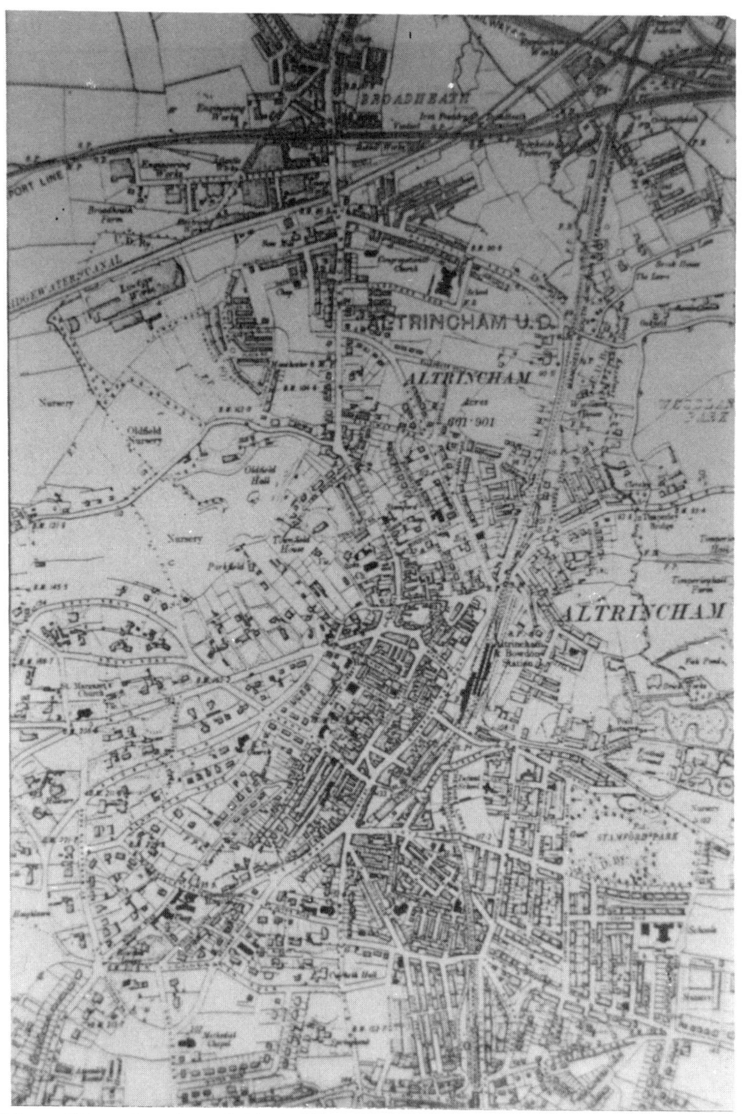

20. Map of Broadheath and Altrincham in 1910 shows the industrial area before the arrival of Record Electrical and Budenbergs. In the north-west is H W Kearns' engineering works. To the north of the railway the new Tilghman building was being constructed where the name Engineering Works appears. On the south side of Atlantic Street to the west are Charles Madan and Castleton Steam Packing.

connections between the interests of the two companies, culminating in a bitter legal dispute over patents in 1920.

J W Record Co (later Record Electrical) (1911)
producers of high quality measuring instruments. Their famous graphic recorders achieved a high reputation as some of the most sensitive in the world. The ingenious idea which started it all was the brain-child of a young instrument designer, Mr John Record, who hit upon the idea of an instrument which recorded (yes, the name was a coincidence) over three-quarters of a circle instead of the one quarter achieved by existing measuring instruments. He called it 'Cirscale' and with it founded the firm which became a famous name in industry. In 1911 he built a small works in Atlantic Street, many times expanded since.

Budenberg Gauge Company (1913)
The Schaeffer Budenberg Gauge Company was founded in Magdeburg, Germany in 1850. Soon one of their most important markets was the Lancashire cotton industry. They opened a sales office in Manchester in 1857 and the first Budenberg (Arnold) came to England. Business rapidly increased until it was necessary first to assemble gauges in Manchester and then to manufacture them in premises in Whitworth Street. As business expanded, bigger premises were needed for which space was not available locally, so the move to Broadheath was made in 1914. The new factory opened with 100 employees with the name Budenberg Gauge Co Ltd, occupying a site alongside Linotype on Woodfield Road, south of the canal. Their building was and remains most attractive. Immediately after the declaration of war, the factory was taken over by the British Government for whom Mr Christian Frederic Budenberg managed the plant. He was known as 'Mr Fred' by his workpeople. Two of his sons served in the British forces. One won the Military Cross; the other was killed in April 1918.

So by 1914, after thirty years, some fourteen companies were established in Broadheath. In some of the more important ones there was a strong American influence and in one of them an original German ownership. Undoubtedly, these overseas connections reflected the declining position of British industry in the period after the era of textile domination.

IV
BRITAIN AFTER THE GREAT WAR

Inevitably a great war lasting over four years involved a great diversion of resources from the pattern previously established. The metal-using and engineering industries, including machine tools and measuring instruments, were greatly stimulated. There was an unprecedented realisation of production potential in meeting the demands of the war machine despite all the problems of wartime production and shortage of manpower. The quantitative stimulus was accompanied by qualitative improvements in terms of new engineering processes and techniques.

A major impact on industry came from the Government, an entirely new development in a private enterprise culture. The Department of Scientific and Industrial Research was established to sponsor research not only in universities but also in industry. Some completely new industries, mainly with a high scientific content, had to be established particularly to replace imports from Germany. The Government even interfered in industry to encourage or impose improved processes and rationalisation as well as to introduce up-to-date accounting practices. All this was disturbing to the old nineteenth century certainties.

One of the principal certainties destroyed by the war was the stability of the exchange rates of the major national currencies which had been tied to the gold standard for most of the century. It is almost true to say that no one engaged in international trade had given a thought to any risk that the currency values in which they dealt could be subject to variation. Certainly there was no question of devaluing or revaluing sterling. True, Joseph Chamberlain had espoused the cause of tariff protection at the end of the nineteenth century but made no progress except to display a sign that the old free trade certainties were being questioned as British trade dominance was threatened by other countries protecting their own burgeoning industries.

Certainly the substantial damage to the established fabric of international trade inflicted by the war in Europe and the activities of the U-boats caused even the gold standard to fall. British exports fell substantially but the need for imports of food and raw materials did not, and a major trade deficit emerged.

The demands for sterling fell quite sharply and the gold standard was effectively abandoned with sterling falling by some 20% by the end of the war. The value of the currency was to become a major issue in economic policy in the inter-war years.

The British non-textile industry was largely strengthened during the war, compared with the damage inflicted on our near continental rivals. With the new recognition arising from the war situation of the vital importance of the major industries of the country as national assets, one might have supposed that a wise government, after the war, would capitalise on the new opportunities offered for the revival of Britain's trade position with a stronger industrial base. How unwisely these opportunities were to be squandered we shall see.

There was, in fact, a widespread failure to appreciate how much the economic world had changed.

The immediate post-war world boom, made inevitable by the rebound from wartime shortages and restrictions, was quickly followed by a slump with the economies of many countries in chaos and currency exchange rates in turmoil. The pre-war certainties based on the gold standard had shattered. So it is perhaps not surprising that British policy, from the end of the war onwards, strongly favoured the restoration of the gold standard. What is rather more difficult to understand in retrospect is why the authorities insisted on trying to restore it on a basis which would effectively increase the value of sterling back to its pre-war parity of almost five US dollars, an increase of some 25% from the level to which it had fallen during the period of 'floating' in 1919.

The reasons for this policy cannot be fully explained here but they had much to do with national prestige and the restoration of an atmosphere of confidence (so beloved in the City) coupled with the feeling that justice should be done to the rentiers (lenders) from pre-war whose returns were fixed in terms of sterling. To justify such an increase in sterling value it was necessary to pursue a policy of deflation so as to reduce sterling prices. Inevitably this process caused many problems, especially as falling prices are not conducive to business enterprise.

The final stage was reached in 1924-25 when a 10% increase in sterling was still necessary to reach the pre-war target. The whole process was hotly opposed by Keynes particularly in his pungently worded diatribe *The Economic Consequences of Mr Churchill* – i.e. Winston Churchill, Chancellor of the Exchequer. More recently, we have become more familiar with the economic consequences of an over-valued currency (for example, in 1980-81 and 1990-1992), so Keynes's patient explanation of the implications of a further 10% reduction in sterling prices of our exports sounds perhaps all too obvious. Of course if prices are to be forced down within the country, Keynes explained, it is necessary to drive down wages first and expect the workers to take the promised fall in prices on trust. He also explained that deflating the economy is achieved basically by creating unemployment.

Undoubtedly this policy was a recipe for disaster, leading to a major coal strike and then to the General Strike of 1926. The more enduring consequence was that Britain lost out by not participating at all fully in the world economic recovery which lasted until 1929. Unemployment which rose to an early peak of 16% in 1921 in the post-war slump, fell to 11% before the return to the gold standard in 1925 which sent it back over 14% by 1930. (These are the official percentages of insured workers; for the total workforce, the figures are estimated to be 25-30% lower.)

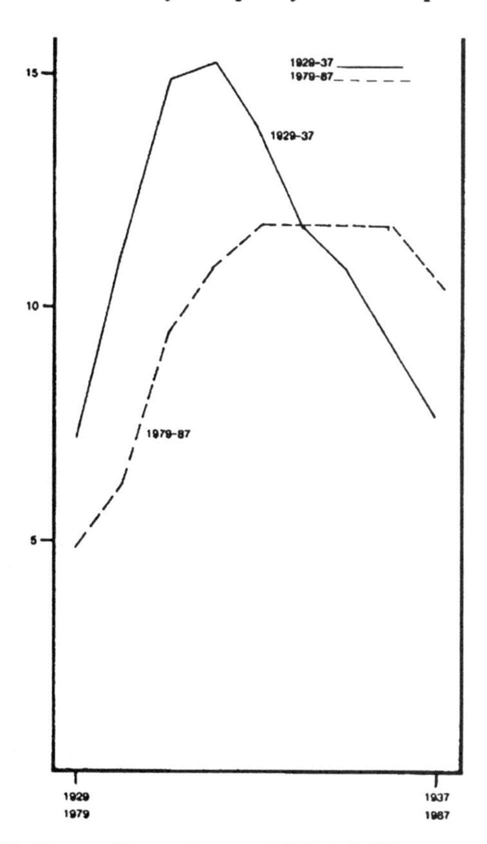

21. Figure: Unemployment 1929 to 1937 compared with 1979 to 1987.

Note: the criteria involved were not the same in the two periods, but the broad picture is probably reasonably accurate; however, the definitions of 'unemployed' in the 1979-87 period were changed many times in ways which tended to reduce the figures over the period. (See Chapter X.)

Industrial production, which by 1924 was perhaps 5-10% above the pre-war level, increased a further 10-15% by 1929, and then fell back to the 1924 level in 1931.

By this time, however, the country was in the throes of the deep world-wide slump which followed the US stock market crash of 1929.

After a minority Labour Government had resisted the devaluation of sterling, the National Government of 1931 abandoned the gold standard to reduce the value of the currency by 25%. Many protectionist and interventionist measures were taken to revive British industry and in 1932 bank-rate was reduced to 2%. A steady recovery then followed to a peak in 1937 when industrial production had increased about 50% above the 1931 (and 1924) level. Unemployment fell to 12% of insured workers compared with over 22% in 1932.

Export business had suffered badly until 1931 because of the overvaluation of sterling. When new policies were applied by the UK Government in the 1930s, the world had become very protectionist so our export business had little chance to revive significantly. However, import prices had fallen substantially in comparison, particularly of foodstuffs, so the standard of living of people in work, assisted by technological progress, increased markedly during the inter-war period – by some 30% between 1913 and 1938. By then Britain was producing less than half its food requirements.

The fortunes of individual industries varied widely. By 1930 cotton textile production was down to less than half its pre-war level. All the major earlier industries, including iron and steel, ship-building and the older engineering industries suffered substantially and were the subject of Government regulation or assistance.

However, the now irresistible forces of technological invention and development were radically changing the world both economically and in consumption. Indeed, industrial enterprise now had to apply itself to the development of new technology as never before, with the Government playing a stimulating and supporting role. Perhaps the most significant underlying change was the exploitation of electricity which transformed most industrial production and promoted new vital trades such as electrical engineering.

The major newer industries which developed quite rapidly in the 1930s under the protection of import duties and on the basis of near-monopoly and cartel organisation were road vehicles, chemicals, man-made fibres (using cellulose), soap and glass.

Where then had Britain arrived at as the Second World War approached? Obviously it was in a very different situation from that which the country occupied in 1914. The once proud workshop of the world with a vast export trade was reduced to being a modest member of the community of nations, all looking after their own interests on the narrowest of fronts, retreating into self-sufficiency as the safest of havens amid the foul winds of international trade. Even so, we were still one of the largest exporters of manufactured goods, second only to – yes, Germany. This was a mark of how far we had yet to fall before, fifty years later, Britain was not a net exporter of manufactures at all.

In terms of technology and organisation, the country's industries were still well behind those of at least Germany and the USA despite some encouraging developments. In terms of education and training, the country's people were poorly provided, in both quantity and quality which were related essentially to the elitist classical education of the few and the neglect of the vast majority. There was substantial disregard of not only technology but also of the science and practice of management of industry.

The moneyed classes, many of them living on the easy money of the nineteenth century, were not very interested in the business of making goods in the twentieth. For gentlemen, the more suitable occupations were the professions, the civil services, including the imperial service, the church, and as time went on, more and more in the City.

In his most valuable book *The State We're In*, Will Hutton has recently emphasised the transformation brought about in the late 1930s as the result of the report of the Committee on Finance and Industry earlier in the decade. The new industries of chemicals, electronics, aerospace and cars were promoted by "twenty years of cheap money; important reforms in the financial system; the first purposeful Government and banking intervention since the Industrial Revolution" involving the "antithesis of the free market orthodoxies of the previous century" – "During the Second World War there was unprecedented direction of capital and state encouragement of investment".

The Committee on Finance and Industry had emphasised the advantages of the "great American and German competitors who are generally financially powerful and closely supported by banking and financial groups with whom they have continuous relationships". So the British banks were pressed for a while to support British industry – to a limited extent. Cheap money was also very helpful, related to the fact that the overseas demands for loans from Britain fell markedly. "Gentlemanly capitalism", wrote Hutton, "its values and its institutions had never experienced such an assault in 150 years."

The Second World War saw the process intensifying with British inventiveness finding strong Government and financial support. According to Hutton, "Production in the key sectors necessary to the war effort increased hugely. The machine tool industry, woefully neglected by the City, saw its output increase five times between 1935 and 1942..."

So, in the later 1930s, the Government's economic recovery programme and rearmament provided new encouragement for British industry, including the Broadheath companies, after a turbulent and depressing period during which most businesses had struggled in conditions of novel uncertainty and difficulty.

V

BETWEEN THE WARS IN BROADHEATH

It is readily understandable that the engineering companies of Broadheath were all heavily involved from 1914 to 1918 in producing the weapons and machinery of war. Undoubtedly, they profited from these activities both financially and from the general boost to their experience and activity. Thus they were well placed to take advantage of pent-up postwar demands. However, in contrast to what happened after the Second World War, business expansion was severely interrupted very soon by a post-war slump, the return to the gold standard and by the huge depression of the early 1930s.

During the war the Budenberg factory was fully engaged in production of essentially the same items as in peacetime, and particularly of pressure gauges for aircraft brakes and for hydraulic operating systems. They were thus in an excellent position to take advantage of heavy post-war demands. Soon after the war ended the Budenberg

22. Budenbergs in 1995.

factory was bought from the Crown by 'Mr Fred' and his family, creating a British company completely independent from its German parent.

After some initial problems because of their German origins, the company established the name of Budenberg in the markets of the world for high quality pressure gauges and many similar products including dial thermometers and various kinds of valves. Next to the watch, the pressure gauge is the most abundant of instruments. The Budenberg company has always aimed at the top end of the market including custom-built gauges.

The market for gauges is comparatively robust, partly because of the wide-range of applications and partly because gauges wear out in use so that there is always a large replacement demand, whereas machine tools, major products of Broadheath, are rather more geared to new investment projects. This market factor may be one reason why Budenbergs have been comparatively successful in surviving the vicissitudes of the national economy. In the inter-war period they experienced considerable problems during the great slump of the early 1930s, but thereafter the business prospered well, so that in 1936 the company built an extension back towards the canal.

Another reason for the continuing success of Budenbergs was probably their emphasis on employing and training highly qualified staff to whom they offered stability in terms of long term employment both before and after the Second World War. Being a private family business they tended to treat employees almost as members of family. Up to a point they could afford to absorb economic and financial shocks. They were certainly prepared at times to carry large stocks of materials and products.

In 1919, there arrived at Broadheath one of the most important and largest employers – Churchills. Charles Churchill was born of English descent at Hampden, Connecticut in 1837. His father was an engineer. When he was twenty-five Charles came to England to install his father's machinery for braiding the steel wires to support crinolines.

While he was in England, Churchill met his friend Hiram Maxim who was engaged on work connected with his Maxim machine gun. It appears that on several occasions he asked Churchill to bring machine tools from America which were unknown in England. The Americans had apparently developed more automatic tools because, it was said, they were at that stage short of engineering craftsmen.

In the event, Churchill saw the opportunity to establish a profitable

23. A Churchills' heavy plain grinding machine built in 1914. (From company brochure, 1956.)

business importing American engineering equipment. The importing business began in 1865 and by the end of the century it had reached such proportions that a factory for 'tooling up' the imported machines was essential and in 1901 a small works was bought in Salford. The need for bigger premises prompted a move to Pendleton in 1904. In 1906 the Churchill Machine Tool Company was formed to design and manufacture machine tools.

The First World War stepped up demand for Churchill machine tools to immense proportions. A site was purchased from Lord Stamford in 1918 and the building of a new factory began the following year. The company's plant soon occupied a vast site on the north side of Atlantic Street, at what was for many years the westernmost edge of the estate. Across the street a similar area was taken up by the company's social club and playing fields. In all the company eventually owned 22 acres.

However, it seems that the first flush of business after the war did not last very long. A booklet produced to celebrate the Golden Jubilee of the company in 1956 told something of the earlier period. After the 1914-1918 war, it reported, indiscriminate sales by the Government of war-used machine tools "knocked the bottom out of the market" for new machines. By 1924 the entire industry was fighting for its existence.

In 1931 there were severe financial problems associated with the national economic crises, the decision to leave the gold standard and the collapse of the stock market. Only by 1934 did the engineering trade began to recover from the trade slump which had begun in the 1920s. Nevertheless, during the whole period, Churchills, it claimed, continued its pioneering work in precision grinding in such spheres as the application of hydraulic mechanisms, and, in 1928, the introduction of the centreless grinder, using some American technology.

Another newcomer to the area in 1919 was ASCO. It appears that seven or eight years earlier a young salesman in Manchester, one Thomas Barrett, had decided that instead of importing a weighing machine from the USA he would manufacture his own. So in 1915 the Automatic Scale Company was founded and after the war it moved to Broadheath to a site in fact not in Atlantic Street but in the north towards West Timperley Station.

The machine in question was one with a visible dial, previously unknown in Britain where shopkeepers had so far used balance scales. In 1922, Thomas Barrett's importing contract expired and the Broadheath premises, which had at one time been a car repair shop, swung into full time production. The company was rapidly expanding. Very soon 100 weighing machines were being produced every week. In 1923 two company huts were erected and soon after the first main extension of 2000 square feet of factory space was built.

By this time the firm had discovered there was a market for bacon slicing machines, so they extended their operations further. Finally, they came upon the idea of refrigerators which they exported all over the world, under the well known ASCO name. In 1929 they started importing from America again and were selling forty different types of weighing and slicing machines. In 1939 the company switched almost all their production overnight to military production.

So this was a company which did not seem to have been badly affected by the national economic situation. It would seem that they had the fair wind of new business ideas to speed them along. For older companies it was more difficult. The *Altrincham Guardian* throughout 1925 was gently bemoaning the poor state of trade which had markedly worsened after the short-lived boom of 1920. The iron and steel businesses were said to be poor in 1924 with low prices and much foreign competition.

In January 1921, the *New York Evening Mail* published an article written by a Maurice Jay, presumably an American, for circulation among the staff of Linotype Machinery Ltd, which said in effect that most of British industry was in serious trouble, but the Linotype plant at Broadheath was working flat out producing typesetting machines and printing presses. It was recalled that the company had originally been formed by a "group of Britishers" to buy out certain US patents. In 1909 the company had been bought by the American Mergenthaler

Company and in 1921 both the chairman and managing director were American. 2,500 people were employed in the Broadheath plant.

The article explained the generous housing and social provisions for the workers and the far-seeing consultation and profit sharing arrangements. Although most of the workers were in trade unions, the company insisted that everyone had direct access to the management to discuss any problems. In the writer's view, there was "a square deal" with a spiritual and ethical aspect as well as an economic value. He felt he had not only been among workers but also 'big men'! He went on, "If the same spirit were to prevail elsewhere in England, the canker of revolution would not make much headway. In such surroundings, the essential common sense of the English has a chance to recover from the shell shock it received during the war which has left its labour a bewildered seeker after impossible utopias instead of the urgent pioneer that it used to be."

However, at the annual dinner of Linotype Works Officers Association in January 1925, it was said that business had been bad since the war but the company had been able to keep their workers busy whilst other companies were partly idle and unemployment was increasing. 1924 had been their best ever year. The company boasted of keeping 15 acres of manufacturing space going which they claimed to be unique in their kind of business.

Clearly, there was close American control of the company including division of the world market for Linotype machines. The German subsidiary was allocated the markets in its own country, Scandinavia, and Eastern Europe. The US plant supplied North and South America with the Broadheath plant supplying the rest of the world.

Unemployment was certainly acknowledged to be serious and Mr Baldwin, Prime Minister, according to the local newspaper, was accused of being protectionist in his efforts to help industry. In August 1925, there was a new policy of plentiful money and a reduced bank rate. Local Conservative politicians were complaining about the miners and the need to reduce the cost of coal production to boost exports and employment. By the end of 1925 the local paper said that the industrial outlook was better with a number of local works showing increasing activity. But the housing shortage was dire with no firm plans to remove Altrincham's slums.

In view of the seriousness of the inter-war economic problems facing British industry in general and machine tools in particular, it is perhaps not surprising that few new companies came to Broadheath

24. H W Kearns' plant in the 1920s.

25. Double spindle horizontal boring machine – H W Kearns.

and none of major importance. In his 1935 book *Bygone Altrincham,* Charles Nickson listed the following operating companies, in addition to those we have already noted as arriving by 1919:

Meldrum Bros – general engineers
Blackwells and National Roofing Ltd – roofing felt manufacturers
Alliance Colour and Chemical Co – airline colour manufacturers
Frederich J Hampson – malting manufacturers
Sherratt & Hughes – printers
Charles Price & Sons – engineers
Lancashire Road Roller Co Ltd

Nickson estimated that 4,000 to 5,000 people were employed in Broadheath factories in addition to "many others engaged in different minor industries".

The columns of the local newspapers in the mid-1930s contain surprisingly few references to the industrial estate, although there are frequent complaints about national economic problems often condemned in editorial solemnity worthy of *The Times*. In 1931 before the formation of the National Government there were sustained criticisms of Philip Snowdon, the Labour Chancellor, for his refusal to help industry as he stubbornly maintained his 'free trade' policy beloved by his Liberal allies.

However, in 1936 the *Altrincham Guardian* did publish a series of articles about Broadheath which enable us to perceive a kind of snapshot of the position after the estate's first half century. The introductory article is headed "MOSS TO MECHANICS" followed by "HEATHER AND LIZARDS SACRIFICED TO MACHINERY". It is confidently stated that the history of Broadheath over the fifty years explains the reason for the continued prosperity of Altrincham "which is one of the most modern and model engineering centres of its kind to be formed".

Whilst market gardening survived to a remarkable extent and vegetables, fruit and flowers left the district daily for Manchester markets, "Broadheath is from day to day becoming more and more dedicated to the insistent demands of a mechanical age. Old established firms are even at the moment extending their borders and good building sites are attracting new enterprises."

With a slightly nostalgic regret for the previous landscape, the writer notes that soon a 60-foot arterial highway would cleave its way through the town and form an effective barrier between industrial Broadheath and residential Altrincham. Yet there was 'romance' to be found in the factories and indeed,

> "amid all the grime and clatter and the grumblings of many folk, some discontented with their lot in life, there is a surprisingly happy outlook among the majority of the 4,000 to 5,000 work people and a smile is far more frequent than a show of temper. It was with these people, upon whom Altrincham largely depends for its prosperity, that I talked and learned of many things that I had not previously known and which made me reflect that, possibly, the growing and continuing murmuring about rates of pay were, perhaps, not absolutely as unmerited as would appear on the surface."

In a later article, the same reporter writes of the attractions of the "bevy of beauties" who walk from the factories at noon or tea-time, side by side with men in grimy overalls. "There is variety in plenty, ranging from golden blondes to brunettes, and from Eton crops to the more fashionable 'long bob and roll!'" The girls were fashionably dressed, they seemed "to have the amazing gift of always appearing in the height of fashion, even when attending to their work! Many smocks hide dresses which would not disgrace a person taking tea at a popular cafe." Even more "the Altrincham girl frankly admits she regularly attends the theatre and unblushingly states that she follows her favourite film star"!

Further articles reported on the business of individual companies. Linotype were employing some 2,000 people in all, including 1,600 'engineers', with an annual payroll of £300,000. They had great difficulty in obtaining skilled workmen despite an extensive apprenticeship scheme. One of the main reasons for the success of the firm was said to be the fact that it had always had the interests of its employees deeply at heart. The extent of the sports and club facilities was of course quite remarkable, as well as a works society, a highly efficient first-aid and ambulance service, a large number of allotments let to employees at nominal rents, meals provided in a canteen at cost and even a guest house for entertaining home and foreign customers.

The chairman of Linotype, Mr Victor E Walker, took a guardedly optimistic fine about business prospects – "In spite of the many difficulties which at present surround a manufacturing business such as ours." There were financial and economic restrictions in a large number of the countries of the world to which Linotype exported machines. So overseas trade was immensely difficult – more difficult than it had ever been. But in the UK there had been, in the past one-and-a-half to two years, a strong forward movement. Overall the company had not only succeeded in improving and developing their plant, but had increased their business.

There was indeed a shortage of mechanics who "are being absorbed in other directions". However, "Our factory is full of work" and the efforts of all its staff were "working in a way that cannot give anything but supreme satisfaction... and which is worthy of all praise".

The *Guardian* reporter had for years known the Radium factory as "the old blacking works", but on his visit there he marvelled at the cleanliness of all the rooms. Mr Harry Lord had emphasised the fact that every endeavour was made to ensure the most perfect working conditions.

Radium were making cleaning products including boot, floor, furniture metal, silver and grate polishes and all kinds of leather dyes and dressings. The associate company, Lord Bros., were making a great variety of tin containers, with each machine set turning out between 12,000 and 15,000 tins per day – and there were eight sets! Further extensions of capacity were planned.

It was reported that there was general satisfaction that the employees were not on piece work. Although a close watch was kept on the actual output and a certain standard maintained, everyone in the works received a regular and stabilised weekly wage. Emphasis was also placed on continuing process of improvement with new devices and machines being developed by the Lord brothers.

The Churchill Machine Tool Company had recently supplied the largest roll grinding machine in the world to Edward Lloyd Ltd for their Kemsley Mills. This machine was being used to grind the rolls of the world's largest newsprint machine at Lloyd's.

For the last eleven years the company, with some 1,100 employees, had had full day and night shifts of workpeople who were also engaged on overtime. The factory, which was at that time still the furthest along Atlantic Street, had green fields on three sides including an extensive sports ground. In the main premises there were eleven bays, occupying 80,000 square feet. Each bay had an overhead travelling crane with a lifting capacity of up to 10 tons. There was also a machine shop under a different roof.

Churchills claimed to have the largest works in the world equipped solely for the manufacture of grinding machines which were supplied to industries in almost every part of the world – including motor vehicle, aeroplane, railways, peppermills, sheet metal mills, printing machinery, ground bar stock, all branches of the electrical industry, marine engineers and many other specialised fields. As a finishing operation the grinding process required accuracies of two ten-thousandths of an inch or less. Several of the smaller plain grinding machines and the internal grinders were worked automatically, the operator merely having to insert a piece and remove it when the cycle of operations was complete – to one ten thousandth of an inch.

The company also claimed to be ousting its American rivals and to be steadily capturing the trade not only of this country, but of the world. Each year they used 5,000 tons of iron and steel in making machines. Some of the grinders themselves weighed 50 tons. Fitters were sent to many parts of the world to supervise the erection of the machines. The company had no foundry but many of the castings were made by George Richards and Company. A special branch railway line ran into the works.

Another article in the *Guardian* in 1936 recalled the foundation of the Thornton-Pickard Manufacturing Company in 1888 and its arrival in Broadheath in 1893. The article credits the Pickard family with a number of developments including one which originated speed photography, i.e. the introduction of the focal plane shutter, a type of instrument used almost without exception in the 1930s for press photography. This was made possible by the invention of an adjustable slip adjustment.

The secretary and joint managing director in 1936 was Mr W G Biddle who joined the firm as an office boy on 1899; he was also a prominent member of Altrincham Borough Council and Mayor of the Borough in 1939. The works manager, Mr F Slinger, had been with the company even longer – for forty years in fact. Quite a number of employees had been on the books for over thirty years.

The article recalled that in 1915 Thornton-Pickards had been requested to make aeroplane cameras for what was then the Royal Flying Corps. They had remained Government contractors ever since.

The company did not make lenses but only the metal and wooden parts of cameras, fitting into them all the well known makes of lenses. Originally, they had concentrated on making shutters but had developed into cameras including the well-known Ruby series.

Because of the seasonal nature of the camera trade, the company had diversified into children's toys and, specifically, by the invention of Mr Gary Pickard, the current chairman, of the brick building-set known as Picabrix which enjoyed great popularity among children of all classes, including those of the Princess Royal, as she declared during a visit to Altrincham in 1928.

Mr Pickard, like other local industrialists, professed optimism about the trade revival, saying that his company was far busier than it had been for some years .

The firm of Luke and Spencer, another of the very early Broadheath arrivals, also seemed to be thriving. Its managing director, Mr William Waterhouse, had been Mayor of Altrincham for five consecutive years, and in 1935 he had been elected vice president of the Abrasive Industries Association.

The *Guardian* article related a familiar, possibly apocryphal, story of the 'olden days' about one of the original founders of the company, Mr

Luke, who was in the habit of returning to his home on the Firs (in Bowdon) in a hansom cab. One evening on arriving at his house, Mr Luke turned to say goodnight to the old driver and to his surprise found the seat empty. After a search 'old John', as he was known, was found on the Downs, having fallen off apparently while asleep. Evidently the horse knew the way home.

The firm specialised in the manufacture of abrasive wheels and grinding machinery which, again in the 'olden days', was done by chipping and filing, but it was achieved in 1936 by abrasive wheels running at a speed of 5,000 feet per minute – or about 60 miles an hour. Indeed the "growing desire for high speed" had led to special wheels being capable of up to three times that speed. The wheels, originally made from natural abrasives – emery and carborundum – were now more often employing artificial abrasives. They ranged in size from a quarter of an inch up to 50 inches in diameter and weighing a ton.

The company had expanded its premises in 1905 and 1915 and more building operations were in hand in 1936. Further, an additional site known as 'Hulberts Mill' had been acquired. The firm had the reputation of looking after its employees well – one indication being that the land adjoining Altrincham Bridge on the main road had been formed into a bowling green. Many employees could boast of thirty or forty years' service and some who were with the firm when it was in Ardwick persisted in travelling daily from Manchester.

The final article in the newspaper series reflected one of the newer companies in Charles Nickson's list – Blackwells and National Roofing Ltd which apparently was situated far to the west in fields near Oldfield Brow. The firm manufactured roof feltings, damp courses and underlinings with fibre, hessian and lead bases. In 1935 "millions of square yards of felting" were made and in 1936 the figure would be almost doubled. Sixty factory workers were employed in addition to "considerable office staff". Expansion was still going on.

A contract had recently been secured for covering the new dock sheds of the Southern Railway with special reinforced hessian-based felting of an untearable nature. Specially hardened felts were used for work in the tropics.

The reporter reflected that after his visit to the plant "it was pleasant to step into the atmosphere of the countryside again and take deep breaths of fresh, clean air. My appearance, despite the protecting overalls, was like that of a tramp who had walked for miles on a summer's day along a dusty lane."

Clearly this local newspaper account of many, but not all, of the major Broadheath companies demonstrates that much of the pessimism engendered by world depression and over-valued sterling in the period up to 1931 had been overcome as a result of general economic recovery and more expansionist government policies, including a more sensible value of the pound. All trades were feeling the benefit, from the highly technological machine tools industry to the more straightforward production businesses – making tin cans or roofing felt, for instance.

Of course, one must not take too seriously these press reports, based as they must have been on information provided by individual companies who would normally tend to show a happy public relations face. One of the companies in particular, i.e. Thornton-Pickard was obviously doing less well than indicated, since they went out of business three years later.

Moreover, a local newspaper reported in 1980 that in 1936 Mr McGuinness, managing director of Churchills, faced with the British Government's unwillingness to under-write orders from the USSR, went himself to Russia and brought back many orders which he shared with Kearns, Richards, Tilghmans, Budenbergs and Linotype.

26. Record Electrical Company: development of factory 1911-1937. (From company brochure, 1937.)

27. Record Electrical Company: calibration of commercial instruments. (Company photograph, pre-1939.)

These orders provided work for many months and were paid in cash. Without them, it was said, all Broadheath would have been unemployed.

This recollected view may well have been more pessimistic about the 1936 (perhaps it was a year or two earlier) situation just as the contemporary press accounts were somewhat optimistic. In general it does appear that there was a slow improvement in business and Luke and Spencer at least were expanding their premises in 1936. As rearmament gathered strength there was going to be additional business particularly for machine tools which still dominated the Broadheath scene.

The Record Electrical Company had, like others, benefited greatly from the First World War. The demand for instruments enabled it to expand its factory total area, particularly for D C instruments for the Admiralty. By 1920 the use of elctricity was growing rapidly and there was a demand for stricter testing of electrical installations resulting in the company's designing a range of insulation test sets. Later it moved into tachometry for use on ships and machinery of all kinds.

However, the company's rate of expansion was not very rapid until

28. Record Electrical Company: machine shop, 1930s. (Company photograph.)

29. Record Electrical Company: bike shed, 1930s. (Company photograph.)

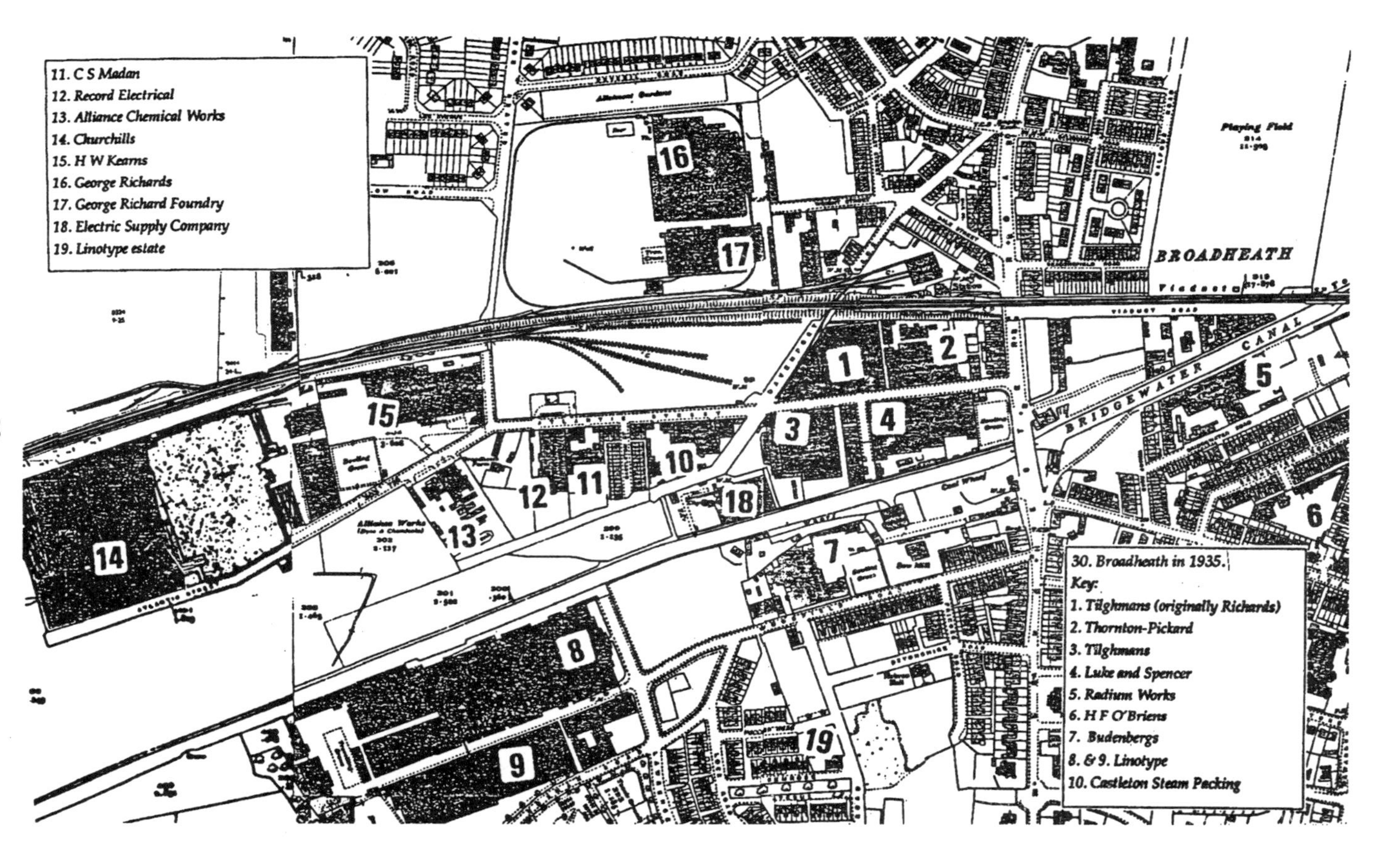
11. C S Madan
12. Record Electrical
13. Alliance Chemical Works
14. Churchills
15. H W Kearns
16. George Richards
17. George Richard Foundry
18. Electric Supply Company
19. Linotype estate
BROADHEATH
Playing Field
BRIDGEWATER CANAL
Viaduct Road
Alliance Works
30. Broadheath in 1935.
Key:
1. Tilghmans (originally Richards)
2. Thornton-Pickard
3. Tilghmans
4. Luke and Spencer
5. Radium Works
6. H F O'Briens
7. Budenbergs
8. & 9. Linotype
10. Castleton Steam Packing

rearmament began in 1936/37 when it was decided, with government help, to erect a new building for production of aircraft engine speed indicators, transmitters, insulation and bond testers for the RAF. By 1938 the demand increased so rapidly that it was necessary to instal another floor on the building erected a year ago.

Throughout the inter-war period George Richards and Co and Tilghmans remained under common ownership, very largely that of B C Tilghman, the grand-nephew of the principal founder. Until 1934 the accounts of the two companies were merged. According to the minute books of Tilghmans, in 1934 the company was involved in some kind of bankruptcy proceedings, but nothing drastic seems to have happened except that the accounts of the two companies were separated.

The table below shows the profits declared in the minute books from 1930 to 1950. The figures are shown after depreciation, tax, management commission and bonuses on wages and salaries. To interpret

31. George Richards: machine tool MC 35 made in 1939 for John Browns in Glasgow for making propellers for the Queen Elizabeth. (Company photograph, 1939.)

the figures in 1995 terms, it is necessary to understand that the general price level was fairly stable in the 1930s, almost doubled during the war and then rose more gently by another 30% or so by 1950. The 1930s profits figures need to be multiplied by about forty to give a rough equivalence in 1935; and the late 1940s figures by at least twenty.

The table shows very clearly that the combined company was having serious difficulties by 1932-1933, obviously related to the Great Slump. In August 1932 the salaries of directors and staff were reduced on a sliding scale running from a 10% cut for those receiving over £10 per week to 5% for those paid below £4 per week. In this regard, it is relevant that B C Tilghman's salary was £1,500 per annum (about £30 per week) plus 6% of profits in 1933. In the same year the general manager was summarily dismissed and a new man appointed at a salary of £500 year with an indication that this would be reviewed when trade conditions improved.

From other evidence it seems likely that skilled male earnings in the early 1930s were around £3 per week or £150 a year. Normally Tilgh-

Profits of Tilghmans & Richards

Year	Tilghmans	Combined	Richards
1930-31		38,562	
1931-32		27,874	
1932-33		8,032	
1934-35	5,766		4,978
1935-36	9,440		17,633
1936-37	20,679		20,455
1937-38	18,895		43,531
1938-39	14,962		65,230
1939-40	8,459		33,408
1940-41	4,324		20,257
1941-42	2,901		16,205
1942-43	6,889		17,872
1943-44	9,435		21,493
1944-45	9,195		24,700
1945-46	12,332		23,856
1946-47	14,225		31,398
1947-48	32,991		39,124
1948-49	56,372		83,459
1949-50	83,450		98,330

32. Atlantic Street in the 1930s.

mans paid bonuses of up to 10% on all salaries and wages in the early 1930s by allocating half of net profits after tax. In 1933, a quarter of the bonus for 1932-33 was held back because of uncertainty about payment for Russian sales. It was announced that no new bonus would be payable for the time being because of reduced turnover caused by the trade depression. It was also noted that delay by the Government in allowing credit had caused the company to forego an expected contract with the USSR for £100,000. The factory was on short-time and there had been a reduction in the number of men employed. So the idea of bankruptcy proceedings in 1934 seems to have been a possibility.

Even in 1931 there was an outstanding loan of £357,000, with a further borrowing of £150,000 authorised. The loan charge for 1930-31 was £17,850 out of a profit of £37,121, leaving a surplus of £19,271, half of which was paid out as a 12½% bonus on all salaries and wages except those of foundry piece workers.

In passing it is worth noting that the relationship between the pay of the chairman of the company and that of the shop floor worker was one of the order of 10:1, somewhat less than in many companies in 1995.

There are some other interesting aspects of the profit figures in the table. Clearly, by 1936 the separated companies were recovering somewhat. Thereafter, Richards went ahead very fast until 1939 with Tilghmans faltering. During the war both companies were in the doldrums until the post-war boom made them quite profitable.

The two companies were of course in quite different businesses. Machine tools were particularly geared to new industrial capacity, making the Richards business volatile in conditions of slump and boon thus explaining the surge in profits as rearmament resulted in a build-up of industry just before the war and again as the post-war boom took hold. Tilghman's business, on the other hand, was mainly in the field of cleaning tools and equipment – partly, but not by any means entirely, a maintenance process which would tend to be much steadier but which could be deferred in difficult times, including the war. After the war, though, even this business increased substantially, partly no doubt to remedy war-time neglect.

VI
THE BRITISH ECONOMY IN THE AGE OF CONSENSUS

The Second World War was immensely damaging to the British economy. The destruction by bombing, the running down of capital assets and the vast disruption of continuity in production were accompanied by the sales of overseas assets and the accumulation of international debts. It was officially calculated that in order to return Britain to something like a viable life it would be necessary to increase the volume of exports by 75% of pre-war levels by 1950 and this had to be achieved by industries which had been distorted by the war.

There is no space in this book to record how this target was achieved, but achieved it was and in 1950 there was a substantial balance of payments surplus. During the same period a social revolution had been effected by the Labour Government, including the introduction of the National Health Service, the national insurance system and what we now refer to as the welfare state. Full employment was essentially achieved without significant inflation.

What then of the industries which provided all these jobs? It should be emphasised that although the government nationalised some major industries such as the public utilities like electricity and gas as well as coal and railways, and, later, iron and steel, manufacturing industry remained essentially in private hands, working within a diminishing framework of controls. Perhaps progress was somewhat too easy for industry in this period of pent-up demand but in general a good recovery had been made from the war and a reasonable base established for a more normal period of peace. By 1950 industrial production was about a third greater than before the war. Interest rates were around 2½%.

There was some benefit to certain industries during the war period. The 'newer' industries such as engineering, metal manufacture and vehicles, as well as the chemical industries, had been quite substantially revitalised and expanded, and this process was extended into the recovery period. Chemicals were outstanding with a doubling of production by 1950 while engineering and vehicles were about 50% up on pre-war levels with lower employment. Iron and steel were of course still important, albeit with new demands, and kept pace with the general expansion of industry.

The period from 1951 to 1979 has become known as the age of consensus because the social and economic revolution effected by the war and by the post-war Labour Government was not seriously challenged and because all governments in the period for almost thirty years followed broadly similar policies to deal with similar problems. The essential problems which dominated the period were, firstly, the balance of payments and secondly, and increasingly, inflation.

Although the balance of payments was restored to temporary surplus soon after the Korean War of 1951, there was never a sufficient margin of safety to act as a cushion when anything went wrong. The need for a cushion was particularly acute because of the existence of large sterling balances left over from the war and held in London by Commonwealth and other countries who could decide to run them down at short notice.

Inflation was a problem which only gradually crept up on the country after 1951, perhaps related to full employment and the slow realisation by organised labour of the strength of its bargaining power in these conditions. Expectations grew of a steadily rising standard of living based on technical progress and the fruits of large-scale production.

In the early years, however, it was the balance of trade which made the British economy vulnerable to shocks and changes in the world economy. In fact the world economy was evolving quite quickly as the war ravaged countries of Europe and the Far East soon restored themselves. Germany and Japan in particular became ever stronger, as, with determined government planning and support of industry, they organised themselves to meet the requirements of the new economic world. The growing overseas competition in international markets, coupled with the vulnerability of the British balance of trade, led to increasingly frequent and severe problems for sterling.

Already in the mid-1950s the delicate balance was being disturbed and in 1957 the first serious threat of a run on sterling caused the government to put the brakes on the economy with a tightening of monetary policy with the Bank Rate going up from a norm of 2½% to the unprecedented post-war level of 7%.

Thereafter, it began to seem inevitable that every few years a government belief in economic recovery inspired an expansionist policy which soon brought in a flood of imports, causing a balance of payments crisis and the risk of a devaluation of sterling – these were the days of fixed exchange rates. Each time this happened the government reversed course and took measures to depress the economy and to restrict imports.

In 1961 a financial crisis developed requiring international loans of over £1 billion to be taken and the Bank Rate to be raised to 7% to save sterling. By 1964, election year, the whole cycle had been repeated and after thirteen years of Conservative 'stop-go' the incoming Labour Government was obliged to take vigorous action to deal with a record balance of payments deficit. In addition to some tax increases, a 15% surcharge was imposed on all imports of manufactured and semi-manufactured goods, amidst much international opposition.

The weakness of the balance of payments had by now become recognised as chronic, and economic policy had to become more or less continuously depressive and deflationary. The Labour Government had to abandon its expansionary National Plan and sterling was belatedly devalued in 1967 from $2.80 to $2.40 to £1. Britain's competitive position in the world economy was steadily deteriorating, in spite of a striking increase in output of some 3½% per annum. Although by 1967 output per person was 47% above the 1950 level even with shorter working hours, the brutal fact was that our European and Japanese competitors were moving ahead even faster, albeit in some cases from lower base levels. Germany, in particular, had growth rates about twice as high as the UK.

It is not easy to be dogmatic about the reasons for this divergence. Some part of it must be associated with conservative management and trade unions and also with the associated deficiencies in British education and training. The low social and cultural standing in the UK of manufacturing industry as an occupation as well as an object of investment still remained a major handicap.

Certainly it was becoming ever clearer that to some extent low comparative productivity was related to the capital equipment of industry being poorer in the UK and that this was associated with a low rate of investment – some 30-40% below that of Germany and Japan. This in turn was partly historical in its causes but was hardly surprising in view of the 'stop go' action of governments which clearly disrupted the steady expansion necessary to establish confidence as well as the profitability which stimulates new investment and makes it possible. The detachment of the banking system from industry was certainly another factor.

The loss of competitiveness of British industry made it increasingly difficult to maintain the continuous increases in real wages which workers had come to expect. Thus there began a series of attempts to control wage increases either voluntary or compulsory, none of them successful for very long. By 1968 there was a veritable explosion of pay increases. But for nearly twenty years inflation had been no more than the 2-3% level common to many countries. In any event, the sharp increase in pay and prices in the late 1960s was a world-wide development, and, despite its many post-war problems, Britain had chalked up very substantial achievements before facing the additional problems of the 1970s.

By 1970, exports had risen almost threefold in volume compared with pre-war and had doubled even since 1950. The real wages of manual workers increased by some 50% from 1950 to 1970, perhaps two and a half times the pre-war level. Furthermore, the lot of working people was also immeasurably improved by the removal of unemployment as a constant threat – still less than 3% at the end of the period, as well as by the provision of welfare services, including the National Health Service. Primary poverty had almost gone.

Yet, inevitably, there was a general impression that somehow things could be better if only new economic policies could end the long period of 'stop-go'. The Conservative Government under Edward Heath, which was in power from 1970 to 1974, inherited a quite healthy economic situation with some scope for expansion, apart from some pressure of cost inflation. Initially, the new Government's policies were of disengagement from the economy, leaving market forces to control the course of events. All attempts to control wages were ended. Credit controls were relaxed. The rate of interest was left as the only lever to influence the economy with a deflatory policy. This was the age of Selsdon Man!

Within a year and a half, inflation rose to 10% and unemployment was rising towards a million, a fact which Heath recognised as a political disaster, so the policy was swiftly reversed by an expansionary budget. This brought unemployment down by 400,000 by 1974, but as shortages of labour, materials and capacity developed, inflation again became a problem. Attempts to secure voluntary pay restraint failed, so a statutory prices and income policy was introduced late in 1973.

At this point there were two major external shocks to the economy which effectively moved from something of a crisis in 1973 towards something near chaos. Of these two external developments, one, the entry of the UK into the European Community, vigorously led by Edward Heath, was relatively slow to have its effect, particularly in the shape of rising food prices. The other more immediately horrendous happening was the first oil crisis, triggered by the Arab embargo, which led to a fourfold increase in oil prices.

There were devastating effects. The balance of payments moved from quite healthy surpluses of around £1 billion in each of 1970 and 1971 to a deficit of well over £3 billion in 1974, of which over half was attributable to the increased price of oil. Inflation soared to a peak of 26% in 1974/75. The need to control wage increases was even more evident in order to stem the wage/price spiral. Having achieved some success with his wages policy, Heath finally lost his second war with the coal miners, putting the country on a three day week in the process. The argument that the high price of oil justified a higher output and value for coal was used to substantial effect by the miners in their claim for a large pay increase. In any event, Heath lost his appeal to the country and let in a Labour Government once more to pick up the pieces.

The new Wilson government never had a majority in Parliament and had little power to do much more than survive. It did, however, secure a voluntary pay agreement with the trade unions which was quite successful for some years, reducing inflation to a low point of 8% in 1978. Despite turmoil in the world economy flowing from the oil crisis and the induced depression following it, the balance of payments was returned to a surplus of £1 billion in 1978, after absorbing deficits on the oil account running at over £3 billion in the mid-1970s tailing off to £2 billion in 1978 as North Sea Oil began to reduce the need for overseas purchases. The index of industrial production, after falling from 1973 to 1975, rose from 100 in that year to 113 in 1979. Fixed investment in manufacturing industry rose 6½% in 1977 and 8% in 1978. Unemployment fell from 1,567,000 in August 1977 to a low point of 1,238,000 in May 1979.

The years 1976-79 were thus a period of marked recovery for the British economy. The voluntary pay policy had a good deal to do with this, but it was fatally ruptured in December 1978 when the government proposed to withhold contracts from the Ford Motor Company if it broke the wages ceiling. This proposal was defeated on a motion in the House of Commons. This led to a series of 'competitive' pay increases. Finally the pay policy and the Government (now under Callaghan) were destroyed by the latter's attempt to restrict public sector pay increases – already lagging behind the private sector – to 5% when price increases were running at 8%. There followed the 'Winter of Discontent' and the election of the Thatcher government.

This brief review of the British economy from the Second World War to 1979 has necessarily concentrated on the events and periods which were of principal importance to manufacturing industry. Against the background of the seminal forces which conditioned the place of industry in the economy and of the major competitive developments in the rest of the world, manufacturing companies had to endure a series of 'stop-go' measures from the mid-1950s followed by swift changes of policy in the early 1970s, leading into the unprecedented trauma of the first oil crisis of 1974, causing wild inflation and rising unemployment. In turn this was followed, with the help of an IMF loan, by a gentle recovery to 1979 when the pay restraint policy, which had contributed so much to the recovery, itself broke down.

It seems highly likely that individual firms, in addition to coping with developments in their own lines of business, must have had particular difficulty in dealing with the upsets of the first half of the 1970s, leading to the three day week and hyper-inflation. World-wide trading disruption was accompanied by substantial loss of real income by the Western purchasers of Arab oil in the Western world. Price rises and wage claims of the order of 25% in a year constituted a scenario for serious costing and marketing problems as well as, inevitably, difficulties of dealing with trade unions, and there were power shortages. Even good managements must have blanched at the disturbance of well established business patterns. Managements which just about got by in normal times must have had their weakness revealed in all these unusual circumstances.

Nevertheless, if one stands back from the 'Winter of Discontent' and the strikes by public sector workers, the British economy was in reasonably good shape in 1979, especially with North Sea Oil beginning to bring a huge uncovenanted benefit. It is of course true that the preceding quarter of a century had witnessed many ups and downs, many disappointed hopes, many disturbances of economic progress. The problem of inflation and control over pay increases had not been resolved, and we should remember that it had been enormously exacerbated by the oil price explosion following which inflation had been reduced from 25% to 8% in less than four years.

Above all, the growth of economic activity had been broadly maintained over the whole of the period with no sustained downturns. There had been nothing like the Great Depression in the middle of the inter-war period which constituted a long drawn-out interruption to economic growth with a vast loss of national product and unemployment rising to 15%. Full employment had been quite well maintained in the Consensus Years but at the end unemployment had reached a peak of around 6% falling to 5%.

The principal restriction on growth had been the delicacy of the balance of payments situation in the small islands of the UK which were so dependent on international trade including the importation of such a large proportion of their food and raw materials. This major restriction was surely about to be removed by the great North Sea Oil bonanza which would also afford the country a wonderful opportunity to invest in its productive capacity and so to improve its industrial efficiency and competitiveness, increasing exports and reducing imports of manufactured goods. Yet this unique opportunity was spurned.

VII
WAR AND PROSPERITY IN BROADHEATH

The Second World War brought immense disruption to the normal progress of Broadheath with the colossal requirements of the war effort supplanting ordinary trading considerations. The nature of the military impact varied considerably according to the peace-time business of each company.

Budenbergs and Record Electrical, both engaged essentially in the production of electrical measuring instruments, continued to make the same kind of equipment during the war and particularly for aircraft requirements. Budenbergs were especially involved in producing pressure gauges for hydraulic operating systems for aircraft brakes. As we have seen, Record Electrical moved into making air speed indicators and other instruments for aircraft and ships' instruments; new production techniques were introduced.

However, another company in the measuring instrument business, ASCO, who normally made mainly weighing machines, refrigerators and bacon slicers, switched largely to armament production, the only conventional products to come off their assembly lines for most of the war being bacon slicers for the Army and Navy. By the end of the war they had produced 1 million mortar bombs, 14 million aircraft bombs, and 3.5 million bomber components.

During the 1939-45 war, Linotype production was restricted entirely to military and air force requirements. Over one and a half million complete units and parts of howitzers, tank and anti-tank guns, Bren guns, Bofors, Browning guns, twin ant-aircraft guns, aeroplanes, armoured fighting vehicles were manufactured. The work of engineering factories all over the country was co-ordinated by group committees formed of parent assembly firms, of which three were chaired by the chairman and managing director of Linotype, Mr V E Walker. It was necessary for over 1,000 people, mainly women and girls ('dilutees') to be intensively trained to replace men going into the forces. The company was particularly commended in letters from the Director-General of Weapons Production in regard to production, particularly of Bren guns and howitzers and for certain design work.

Contrasting with these companies which were involved in major

33. Sir Greville S. McGuinness KBE, chairman of the Churchill Machine Tool Company speaking to King George VI on the occasion of the latter's visit to Broadheath in 1946 to thank local industry for its immense war effort. McGuinness played a leading part in obtaining Russian orders not only for Churchills but also for other Broadheath companies.

changes to their production lines during the war, the machine tools companies, Churchills, Kearns and Richards, continued to make basically the same kind of products as in peace-time, but of course to somewhat different specifications, in order to equip the great munitions factories. The technical position established by Churchills was such that after 1939 their machine tools played a vital part in the war effort. The workshop of practically every Royal Navy dockyard was equipped with Churchill grinding machines. Although the modern machines had become more and more automatic, the company produced a special gear-driven model for use in the field by the army in North Africa. The most spectacular use of all was in the building of military aeroplanes which required unparalleled accuracy.

When King George VI and Queen Elizabeth came to Broadheath in 1946 to say thank you for the estate's huge war effort, it was the Churchills plant

34. Mr Granville Barlow, the oldest employee, on the same royal visit.

35. One of Churchills's thirteen assembly bays covering altogether 160,000 square feet.

that they particularly visited.

After the war there was, inevitably, a great pent-up demand for the products of all the major companies, whether or not they had made major changes for war production. The more technological businesses had substantial initial advantages because of the devastation of Germany. In general the Broadheath companies emerged from the war in very profitable situations, although, as we have seen, Richards and Tilghmans only moderately so.

Linotype, in particular, after being very modestly profitable in the inter-war period, make very large amounts of money out of their war efforts, most of which had to be remitted to their American owner. In 1945 they found themselves with an immense order book for printing equipment – three or four years' worth for Linotype machines and as much as ten years' worth for printing presses. Churchills, too, were said to be blessed with a great back-log of orders. Whether these were real blessings is arguable. They tended to breed complacency and lack of concern for the medium and long term future.

This kind of neglect is likely to have been potentially hazardous for most of the companies. Life both during the war and for quite a long period afterwards was comparatively tranquil in a business sense. Even bombs had been conspicuously absent for what was obviously a suitable target, albeit a rather small one before the days of precision bombing. Only O'Brien's oil works in Brunswick Road suffered badly, although there was a near-miss by a land-mine, no doubt intended for the industrial estate, which severely damaged an area in Wright Street and Huxley Street, just to the north.

From the commercial point of view, the immediate post-war period was vastly more favourable than the post-1918 years, partly no doubt because the lessons of those years had been learnt to the extent that there was improved national and international economic management. The hidden danger was, as we have suggested, complacency as foreign competition grew apace especially as the defeated enemy countries re-equipped themselves from scratch.

In the early months of 1960 the local weekly newspaper, *County Express*, published a series of articles on the leading Broadheath companies. The following table lists those firms and the dates when they arrived in the area.

Year	Company	Product	No. of Employees
1885	George Richards and Co	Machine tools	?
1897	Linotype	Printing equipment	1700
1898	Tilghmans	Shot-blast and abrasive cleaning equipment	?
1903	Charles S Madan	Pumping equipment	130
1904	Radium Broadheath Ltd	Leather dyes and polishes, incorporating Lord Bros. tin containers	250
1907	H W Kearns	Machine tools	500
1910	Record Electrical	Electrical measuring equipment	600
1914	Budenbergs	Pressure gauges	300
1918	Automatic Scale Co.	Weighing machines	400
1919	Churchill Machine Tool Co.	Machine tools	1100
1950	J P McDougall	Decorating materials and equipment	160
1952	MSP (Luxi-Products) Ltd	Toys, nursery equipment	130

1955	J B Electric	Electrical repair	36
1956	Vicrete Products	Pre-cast concrete products	40
1957	Burn Watson (Navigation Road)	Cleaner compounds	?
1958	P I Castings Ltd	Castings	80

From other information, it is clear that there were also a number of other companies in operation in 1960 including:

Year	**Company**	**Product**	**No. of Employees**
1895	Luke & Spencer	Abrasives	?
1956	Baldwin & Francis, who built a large plant on the south side of Atlantic Street next to the west of the Churchill playing fields	Flame-proof mining and industrial control gear	1000
?	E Boydell & Co	Dumpers, loaders and shunters	?
1956	Broadheath Castings Ltd	Castings	15
	Harland Engineering Co	Centrifugal pumps, hot water circulators	?
?	J F Parker	Scrap metal preparation for industry	?
1894	O'Briens in Brunswick Road	The oil company established	?
1960	Switchgear & Cowans who built a large plant next along to the west of Baldwin & Francis		

(In 1962, the local *Guardian* reported that some other companies were operating in the area including Industrial Colloids in Viaduct Road who "manufacture and introduce colloidal degreasants and detergents to industry". The trade name 'Colosyl' was said to be known all over the world.)

The total number of employees in the firms for which figures are given is 6441. Allowing for the unrecorded figures for Richards and Tilghmans, and for other companies not included in the survey, we must conclude that some 8,000 or more people were employed on the estate and the numbers appear to have been increasing.

The *County Express* indeed records that the estate was still growing. Recently the Altrincham Council had opened a new trading estate where young companies were rapidly expanding. It was emphasised that in general labour relations in the area were excellent. "One never heard of a failure." The original companies continued to flourish. "The atomic age has offered them a new challenge, which they have accepted."

It all sounds incredibly successful and optimistic. Perhaps it was a good thing that these industrialists could not foresee the next twenty odd years.

Of course it was not true, even in 1960, that all the original companies still flourished. At least one important early name had disappeared even by 1939 – Thornton-Pickard. Another half-dozen which were operating in 1935 seem to have disappeared. But the post-1945 period was clearly an expansionary one.

On the other hand, the above list displays an alarming hiatus in the inter-war period, with no company which entered Broadheath between 1920 and 1950 apparently surviving to 1960. Certainly the big important firms had all started business over forty years ago.

Following are some of the more interesting comments made by *County Express* on the individual companies:

George Richards & Co Ltd

The company was engaged in the manufacture of horizontal boring and facing machines, vertical boring and turning mills – from 4 to 50 feet diameter capacity – and planing and cutting machines. This firm was closely linked to Tilghmans in common ownership but operated as a separate company.

Linotype

"Ever since it opened the factory has played a vital role in the life of Altrincham. It has taken its name to every corner of the world. It has brought the town new life. Its fortunes are synonymous with Altrincham's fortunes."

"But it does much more than that. By its manufacture of Linotypes, printing presses and auto plates, it plays its part in the destiny of the world. As nations emerge from the 'dark ages' of ignorance and domination, strive towards self-determination and a status in the world, so do they send their trade missions to Broadheath."

"The light of education spreads among backward countries carried by the printed word. Newspapers and books bring new ideas, new concepts to fire the minds of hitherto illiterate and primitive peoples. Ideals and concepts hammered out on the keys of the Linotype machine are pounded out on its printing presses."

"That is the romance that lies behind Linotype. Its future is the World's future."

60% of the company's products were being exported. With its associated overseas factories, the company covered the world. "Eight different Linotype models, six different types of presses and six types of autoplates and autoshavers are turned out by the 700 people in the Broadheath factory."

There were many drawing offices, the pattern-makers' shop, the four foundries, tool room (where precision work of the highest degree was carried out) machine shops, erecting bays and testing rooms. The company's apprenticeship scheme had been recently extended, widening the scope for promotion. With its generous provision of houses and amenity facilities, the firm had a proud record of good labour relations and had never had a 'private' strike on its hands. During two world wars the whole resources of the factory were turned over to making the instruments of war.

> "Linotype played its part in many battles. But in the years of peace it plays its part in the greatest battle of all... in the progress of nations towards their destiny. Towards a better world."

In the mid-1990s it is hard to believe that such optimistic notes could be struck only a generation ago. An important point is, however, buried in the above comments about the worldwide nature of Linotype's business. The great variety of languages, scripts and symbols did involve a significant penalty in terms of the costs involved in making typesetting machines.

Tilghmans

This company "produce abrasive cleaning equipment, pressure-operated shot-blast plants, air compressors, vacuum pumps, dust extraction plant, conveyors and all abrasives and equipment."

Charles S Madan

This company "manufactures a wide range of hydraulic pumping machines. The machines can squeeze powdered metal into a solid bar. They can also be used for checking steel tubing for strength and finding flaws in oxygen bottles. The firm is the leading manufacturer in the field." Since 1947 they had doubled their factory floor space and their staff. "Their pumps are used all over the world – in the manufacture of paint, textile machinery and in the atomic power field."

Radium (Broadheath) Ltd and Lord Brothers

"Since 1904 when Mr Squire Lord moved his leather dressing firm from Eccles and set up business in an old iron foundry in Bridgewater Road, the premises have been extended five times and cover an area of some three acres – approximately nine times the size of the original site. In 1960 the Radium company manufactured the well known leather and satin dyes, all kinds of leather finishes and household polishes."

Radium had begun manufacturing their own tins for their own products and were so successful that they decided to produce tins for the open market. A separate company, Lord Brothers was formed and "now make the tins for many paint, food, confectionery and chemical manufacturers. Their triangular trade – mark is known to millions and their vans are a familiar sight in all parts of the country." The joint managing directors were the two sons of Squire Lord – William and Harry. "Many of the employees at the factory have been there for over thirty years. They have played a part in one more Broadheath success story."

H W Kearns

"A button is pressed... lights twinkle... ten tons of machinery whirrs into life... and clicks into position within one – thousandth of an inch. And it is all done by buttons. The machine is the pride and joy of the H W Kearns factory. It represents more than half a century of experiment and research." For many years the company had specialised in the production of one machine – the horizontal borer, well known throughout the world. "Their latest model is revolutionary. The company are at the forefront in the development of electronic control."

Sir Lionel Kearns, the son of the founder, who took over as chairman from his father, in 1960 lived in Groby Road, Altrincham. He was knighted during the war when he was director of machine tool production for the Ministry.

Raymond Massey at work in the company's experimental department.

Senior sales representative, Mr Ralph Layland, who has been with the firm for fifty-two years, pictured when he received a gold watch from chairman Sir Lionel Kearns.

Apprentices John Holden, of Millington, and Bill Flisk, of Princess Street, Broadheath, at work in the fitting department.

Mr H Jackson, a designer, and the company's senior demonstrator, Mr Fred Walker, at the controls of the electronic-age machine.

36. Four pictures of H W Kearns from 1960.

"The firm keep a keen eye on their sixty apprentices who move around the various departments during their five year apprenticeship. And one of their machines – the 'S' type horizontal borer – is used in technical colleges throughout the world."

(In 1962 Kearns added a new building adjacent to their main works plus 30,000 square feet of modern office accommodation.)

Record Electrical

This company started fifty years earlier. The first big expansion came during the First World War when it secured several Admiralty contracts. The company was hit by the depression in the early 1930s but after two years of uncertainty started to thrive again with the introduction of the rearmament programme. In 1937 the first 10,000 square foot of factory floor was built and in 1940 a second storey was added.

During the Second World War the factory switched to making air speed indicators for aircraft and ships' instruments. After the war, they established themselves as one of the country's leading manufacturers in their field of electrical measuring instruments for every kind of industry from counting corn to measuring nuclear power. In 1959 they added a third floor to their factory. "The flashing dials and flickering needles of the Broadheath – made instruments were also used when the GPO's cable-laying ship, the *Monarch* laid a new cable across the Atlantic. The Record instruments told the GPO engineers the rate per minute of the cable paid out from the *Monarch*."

In 1957 "the company's main rival – a southern company – took over control. But even after this the family spirit that has been with the firm since the start has not been destroyed." In 1960 the club for employees with more than twenty-five years service had a membership of over a hundred.

Budenbergs

"Next to the watch, the pressure gauge is the most abundant of instruments. And Budenberg gauges are the 'Rolls Royces' among them. The firm specialises in supplying custom – built gauges – and dial thermometers – of the highest accuracy for industry and research."

"A true family firm with a fine record of works management relations never having had an internal strike, with seventy-three employees who have been with the company more than twenty-five years."

"One man who has almost topped the 'twenty-five' mark is Harry

37. One of Budenbergs workshops, 1960.

Potts of Woodfield Road. He is one of the men who has been given the exciting task of going out to Australia to start the new branch of the firm near Melbourne."

The article recalls that the firm originated in Magdeburg in Germany. During the last war the original factory was supplying gauges to German fighters while its Broadheath offshoot was equipping the aircraft of the Allies. Afterwards the German factory was taken over by the Russians and renamed the Karl Marx factory.

In August 1961, *County Express* reported that Budenbergs, needing to expand, had decided to build a plant in Anglesey because of the shortage of labour in the Altrincham area. In fact, the company had sought planning permission to expand their factory at Broadheath, but Mr Freddie Erroll, the local MP, who was Minister for Trade, had persuaded them to invest in the development area in North Wales, and benefit from government incentives.

The Altrincham plant still employed 300 people and was not to be run down. Indeed an extension was soon built eastwards along Woodfield Road so as to provide an improved flow of materials and production.

Automatic Scale Company

The ASCO story, had like many others, started in Manchester. A young salesmen, Thomas Barrett, had decided that instead of importing a new American weighing machine he would manufacture his own. In 1915 the Automatic Scale Company was formed and moved to

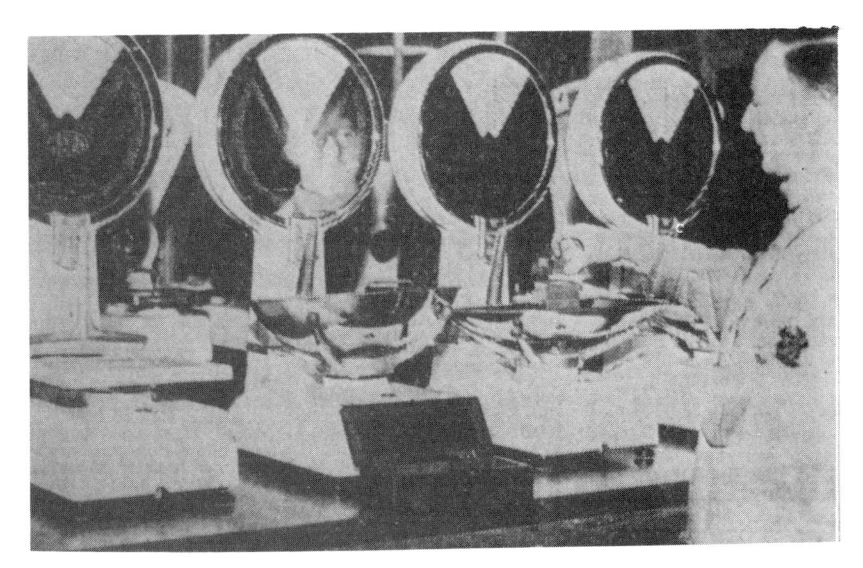

38. ASCO Company weighing Machines, 1960.

Broadheath in 1918.

Since then they had become a famous trade name with forty depots throughout the country and employed more than 400 people. In the inter-war period they diversified into bacon slicing machines and especially into refrigerators which they exported all over the world under the famous ASCO name.

In 1939 the company switched almost overnight to supplying the forces with a bewildering variety of weapons, tools and components. After the war the company switched back to weighing machines and refrigerators.

In 1960 they had 120 'workmen', 50 office staff, 120 service mechanics, 70 salesmen and a fleet of 65 vans.

Churchill Machine Tool Co.

The *County Express* declared, "The history of Churchills is in the history of precision grinding. In the space of fifty years the firm has pioneered the technique from small beginnings to what is today one of the major methods of metal machining. It is the biggest works of its kind in Europe, probably in the world – occupying 10 acres for buildings in 22 acres of land in Atlantic Street and employing 1,100 men. It had its own training school for apprentices. "Here a hundred different types of grinding machines are made, each to be manufactured in different sizes. From here recently went the largest grinding machine Churchills have ever made, weighing 137 tons for a works at Crewe. It could be contrasted to a small grinder that was ordered for grinding valves for the trumpets of the Salvation Army."

"Precision is everything, precision beyond the conception of the man-in-the-street. In a sealed dust-proof room kept at a constant temperature, are machines which will measure to a millionth of an inch." "A thousandth of an inch is parkland."

J P McDougall Ltd

Although it was a limited company, McDougalls remained a family firm originating in a wallpaper business in two cellars in Blackfriars Street, Manchester and becoming the "biggest independent merchanting organisation at the service of the decorator". In 1950 the company came to Broadheath where they cleared a site of derelict buildings and built a new block of modern offices. In 1960 the firm was still expanding at a turnover of over £1½ million a year with 160 employees.

M S P (Luxi -Products) Ltd

This company occupied a one-storey red brick building in Davenport Lane, making toys and nursery equipment.

After being 'demobbed' after the Second World War Mr Smith began making toys in an old coach house a mile further north off the Manchester Road. They graduated to supplying upholstery and bedding for carry cots. Soon they moved to a corner shop in Ashley Road, Hale, and in 1952 they came to Davenport Lane. Since then the turnover had multiplied four-and-half times by 1960. They also had offices in Atlantic Street, an old church in Stockport Road, Timperley, the corner shop and still the old coach house, used mainly as a store room. In all they employed 130 people.

J B Electric

This small electrical repair company employing thirty-six people originated in 1945 in a shop run by the Bancroft family in The Causeway, Altrincham, doing electrical repair work for local firms. When the Altrincham Electric Supply Company decided to change the voltage, J B Electric got the job of re-wiring 3,500 vacuum cleaners in the area.

In 1946 the company moved to premises in Manchester Road and in 1956, employing only bricklayers, the family built themselves their present factory in Atlantic Street – all in eight weeks. In 1960 they were still working day and night on a great variety of repair work – from domestic appliances to generators, transformers and control gear.

Frequently they were called to Salford Docks to work on a ship as it steamed through the Ship Canal, hoping to finish the work before arriving at Liverpool and being carried off to Canada.

Recently the company had turned to making fluorescent desk and wall light fittings, and were thinking of building another factory on adjoining lands.

Vicrete Products (Altrincham) Ltd

Another small company employing forty men which began in 1951 in a small yard in Navigation Road. In 1956 they were given a plot on the new Altrincham Industrial estate. In 1960 they employed a fleet of lorries supplying the North West with products ranging "from gauges to garden paths".

Burn Watson Ltd

"Three times a week for a year, three company directors would meet around a washtub in Broadheath and shampoo their hair." In this manner the company developed a new shampoo for dogs to be made at their premises in Navigation Road. The firm started business in 1957, putting on the retail market many cleaning products which had been used in industry for many years. They had branched out into the pharmaceutical field with a skin treatment, and into the veterinary field. They were still growing in 1960.

P L Castings Ltd

This firm began in 1950 with a pilot plant in the 'sister company' of Charles Madan and Company in Atlantic Street. In 1957 they moved into the shell of a building across the street which in two weeks they turned into a brand new and completely equipped factory. In 1960 they produced over a million castings a year, for use in 150 industries, including garment making and printing. On display at a recent Earls Court exhibition was a knitting machine containing no less than 400 castings designed and produced in the Atlantic Street factory.

The company used a casting technique said to have been invented in the second millennium BC under the Chang Dynasty in China, an age noted for the beauty and skill of its bronze work. The process became known as the 'Lost Wax' – "A model was made of wax, covered with clay. The wax was then melted and drained off and molten metal poured in – thus, the 'Lost Wax'. The result was a casting that betrayed no joins or seams. A perfect casting." The Eros statue in Piccadilly Circus was made by the technique called Precision Investment Casting.

In 1960, some eighty people worked in the factory half of them women whose skilled fingers were necessary for certain processes in production.

General Observations

There is obviously a contrast between the major companies which started business before 1920 and the smaller, mainly family firms, which began operations after 1945. The former were essentially in basic engineering and machine tools, printing machinery, measuring and weighing equipment, shot blasting and pumping machinery, with the rather different one in leather dyes and polishes diversifying into tin containers. The newer firms were beginning to exploit the demands of a somewhat more affluent society – for decorating materials, toys, dog shampoos and the like. However, other companies not reported by *County Express* were engaged in more industrial type operations such as control gear production as well as "dumpers, loaders and shunters", pumps and scrap metal preparation.

Clearly there had been some failures on the estate – a few companies which had started businesses in the inter-war period had not survived – and some of the 1950s companies had taken over old sites and buildings. Yet the general atmosphere was one of success with some expansion. No significant complaints come through – apart from one 1960 report on the deplorable state of the local roads especially Davenport Lane with potholes two feet deep, in respect of which the local companies, the Council, British Railways and the Stamford Estates could not agree responsibility.

Prosperity clearly persisted for most companies through the 1960s. In March 1962 the *County Express* reported Churchills' 'Open Day' when the company boasted of its biggest ever order book and of a break-through into the closed US market with a machine to beat all-comers. In 1966 the company embarked on a planned programme of growth including product development and sales promotion and were planning an additional production unit at Runcorn. Their export business continued to flourish and in 1969 they received the Queen's Award for export achievement and technological invention. In January 1970 they were employing some 1,100 people.

All, however, was not quite as it seemed with Churchills. In 1961 the company was taken over by BSA (Birmingham Small Arms Company), which also had a large manufacturing operation, including machine tools, together with an excellent sales organisation. In 1967, the marchine tools part of BSA was itself takėn over by Alfred Herbert to help fill their order books following a rapid decrease in orders for their own machine tools including capstan lathes, which were said to be out-dated.

It is important to consider the different motives for these two take-overs. The BSA acquisition of Churchills appears to have been a reasonably straightforward endeavour by BSA to broaden their business which became increasingly threatened by Japanese production of motor cycles and cycles. The initial bid by BSA was reported to be worth some £8½ million – probably worth some £150-£200 million in 1995 money, although part of the offer consisted of BSA shares; and these terms may have been improved.

Certainly Churchills did not appear to suffer from the take-over and, as we have noticed, continued to thrive during the 1960s, reporting profits of £344,000 in 1968 and £307,000 in 1969 – of the order of £6 million. Queen's Awards are not granted for temporary freak results, but for sustained performance over a period of years.

On the other hand, some senior Broadheath people from those years have commented that Churchills were too narrowly committed to huge Russian orders, turning away other business. The truth seems to be that Churchills, dominating the supply of UK grinding machines, produced a great variety of shapes and sizes pf machine. In the 1950s and 1960s they were awash with orders – one reports says that there was so much paper that the staff actually threw some of it away! The company's real problem was in making their wide range of machines to meet order dates. There was a procession of works managers, but apart from a period in the 1950s, control of production was inadequate, so with pressure on delivery dates, quality was prejudiced. The design department was active enough, but the flow of new designs tended to exacerbate the production problem. Towards the end of the period, foreign competition was making life harder.

However all this may be, Churchills was an attractive target for Alfred Herbert because of the strength of their order book and general profitability, whilst Herberts themselves were in difficulties in their principal lathe business. By the same token, the increasing market difficulties of BSA may well have prompted them to sell out. The conse-

39. Small Richards boring machine. (From company brochure, late 1940s.)

40. Richards' erection shop for medium size horizontal borers. (Company brochure, late 1940s.)

41. Tilghmans' No. 4 plant housing machine shop, compressor erection, and dust frame division.

quences of all this we shall see a little later.

In the 1950s and the 1960s significant changes were also affecting George Richards, H W Kearns and Tilghmans. During the nationalisation of the coal and steel industries the Staveley Coal and Iron Company received substantial compensation for their assets. They used this money to invest in the machine tool industry, taking over thirty of the most important firms in the country, including Richards and Tilghmans, in the early 1950s.

A newspaper report described the Staveley company as being worth £14 million. The amount they paid was said to be a secret but "must be substantially more than £1½ million", which sounds very low in relation to the £8½ million said to have been offered for Churchills ten years later. Tilghmans were said to employ 1,300 people which may well have included the Richards staff.

It appears that the two principal directors of Tilghmans and Richards, i.e. B C Tilghman and Miss Mathewson, the granddaughter of an early associate of the founder of Tilghmans, had decided to retire and therefore agreed to sell out. There seems to be no doubt that Staveleys made little provision for the development and design of Richards' machines. In the technological business in which German companies were making great strides this neglect was deadly for Richards, especially following a premature move to adopt tape control of production. By the late 1950s, despite certain efforts to redesign their

42. *Kearns-Richards: boring machine, 1970.*

range of horizontal boring machines, it seems that there was a decline in customers' confidence. By 1960, according to Sparkes, Staveleys had decided that Richards needed a stronger management team and were proposing to move the plant and personnel to a new site.

In the meantime H W Kearns was coming to the end of the period of strong family control. In 1955 it became a public company. The death of Sir Lionel Kearns in 1960 brought the changes to a head and there was a new move towards links with other companies. After flirting with an offer from Tube Investments, Kearns, who were still quite profitable and had expanded their premises substantially in 1962, accepted in 1965 an offer from Staveleys who by this time had it in mind to close Richards which was losing money. Within a few months the Kearns directors were replaced and a massive redundancy programme implemented. Most of Richards' operations were transferred to the Kearns building and Tilghmans moved into the Richards' building from Atlantic Street.

Again according to Sparkes, by 1970 both Kearns and Richards were facing total closure. Customer confidence had been severely damaged and orders continued to fall.

Tilghmans had in the meantime become associated with the American Wheelabrator Company from which they had taken a licence in 1936. The US company progressively provided them with finance in return for shares and took them over completely in 1972 and set up subsidiaries in Germany and France in 1968 and 1970. It was said that their compressors were used in a wide variety of industries in the UK and indeed in the world. They specialised in pollution control.

The Linotype Company had also run into difficulties in the 1960s. Their swollen order books after 1945, coupled with the need to remit most of their profits to their US owners, led to a state of complacency and inertia reflected in out-of-date machinery and lack of planning for the future. This situation could in any event have been very dangerous. The development of the photocomposition method of typesetting made it nearly disastrous. Although the resistance of the printing trade unions seriously delayed the use of the new invention in the UK, the writing was very much on the wall and should have been read earlier.

Nevertheless, in the late 1960s, Linotype secured their position to some extent by taking over the only UK company producing the new typesetting equipment in London and moving it to Cheltenham for larger scale production. The new equipment used quite a different technology to the Linotype machine and was essentially simpler. The company would have preferred to make it at Broadheath but was unable to negotiate wage rates for the electrical engineering staff less than about 30% more than they could in the south of England.

It appears that the prevailing wage levels in the Greater Manchester area in general and Broadheath in particular were relatively high at this time, which is understandable given that the late 1960s was the period of peak prosperity in the area and more widely in British industry.

Nevertheless, the Linotype Company itself was remarkably successful in the business of photocompositors, supplying Europe and the British Commonwealth from the UK and establishing production in the USA to supply the rest of the world.

As far as the old Linotype machines were concerned, the business was reduced to servicing them in many countries with a modest and reducing level of supply of new machines.

In the field of printing presses, Linotype took a new lease of life by developing a web-offset machine in the late 1960s which was popular with some newspapers and particularly with the producers of cheap and glossy school books for the Third World.

Thus they were able to keep the machinery side of the Broadheath operation going reasonably well for some time. In the early 1970s, 65% of their total business was for export. But their number of employees at Broadheath fell progressively from some 1,750 in the early 1960s to 600 by the mid-1970s.

So the proud Linotype Company from the last century, having fallen into the hands of an American owner which soaked up its profits and controlled its overseas markets, had done quite well by 1970 to

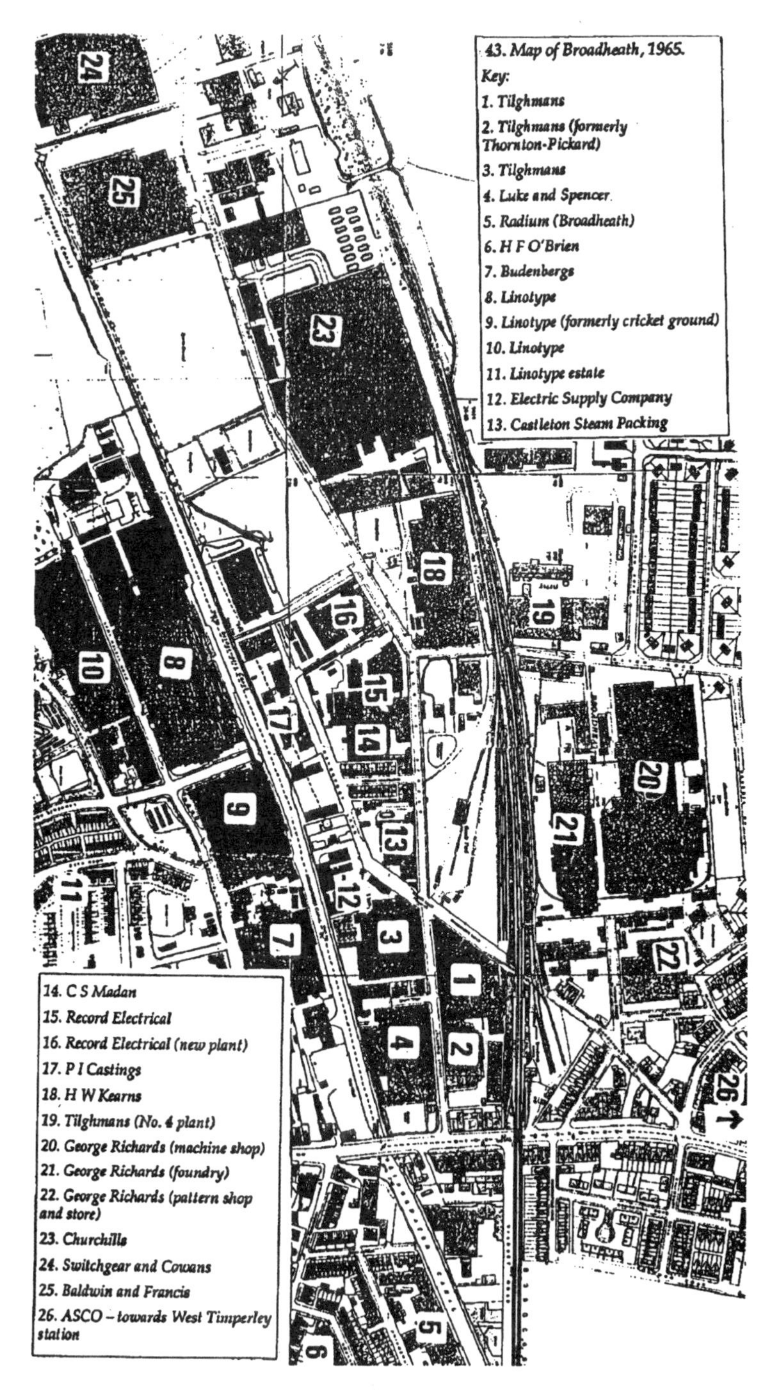
43. Map of Broadheath, 1965.
Key:
1. Tilghmans
2. Tilghmans (formerly Thornton-Pickard)
3. Tilghmans
4. Luke and Spencer
5. Radium (Broadheath)
6. H F O'Brien
7. Budenbergs
8. Linotype
9. Linotype (formerly cricket ground)
10. Linotype
11. Linotype estate
12. Electric Supply Company
13. Castleton Steam Packing
14. C S Madan
15. Record Electrical
16. Record Electrical (new plant)
17. P I Castings
18. H W Kearns
19. Tilghmans (No. 4 plant)
20. George Richards (machine shop)
21. George Richards (foundry)
22. George Richards (pattern shop and store)
23. Churchills
24. Switchgear and Cowans
25. Baldwin and Francis
26. ASCO – towards West Timperley station

rescue itself from the poor position to which complacency and a technological revolution had led it by the early 1960s. In Broadheath, however, there was a major set-back, perhaps epitomised by the fact that the Linotype houses were only 15% occupied by company employees when they were sold off in this period; but this was largely attributable to the changing pattern of occupation through the successive generations.

The generous attitude of the company in respect of welfare provision which had been emphasised from the outset in the late nineteenth century was maintained after the Second World War. A variety of social clubs were organised. Allotments were provided for nominal rents. Employees were assured that they need not worry about sickness – the firm would look after them. The staff handbook of 1973 laid down provisions for sick pay and stated that, after this was exhausted, the company would endeavour to provide continuity of employment. Hours of work were thirty-seven and a half a week for staff and forty for shop-floor workers. There was provision for the hearing of grievances of individuals and groups of employees. A new social club was built in the 1970s.

On the other hand, and perhaps taking account of its welfare provisions, the company was generally known as the low payer of Broadheath, and the staff were aware that much of the machinery, especially in the older parts of the factory, was outdated. Trade union membership was low – including no more than half the employees, and the management's relations with the unions was essentially 'at arm's length'.

In any event, the great technical changes in the printing business made it inevitable that employment at Broadheath would be greatly reduced. A modest proportion could in this period have been saved, or rather replaced, if the trade unions had been more flexible in a period of prosperity.

Thus the somewhat cosy world of Broadheath, in fair part dominated by family companies, was being invaded by powerful external forces. In these peak years of the mid-to-late 1960s some 9,000 to 10,000 people were employed on the estate, but the scene was being set for the trauma to follow.

VIII
1970S – DECLINE AND HOPE

If the 1970s started badly with the decline of Richards and Kearns, they were to get worse before they got better. One major problem concerned Churchills, the other company taken over by people who did not know the business.

At the very beginning of 1972, the Alfred Herbert Company announced that it was closing the Churchills plant at Broadheath within a year. About 1,100 jobs would disappear, although a few men would be offered work at their Coventry factory to which the Broadheath equipment and orders would be transferred. The company was clearly short of work overall and they needed to close one of their four plants "to save capital expenditure". After careful consideration, the Altrincham plant had been selected as the victim.

There was uproar locally at this announcement. There were demonstrations, marches through the town and even strong support for the workers by Altrincham Council. The unions threatened to prevent the transfer of machinery and work to Coventry, although operating the Broadheath factory normally. There were deputations to local MPs Anthony Barber, who was Chancellor of the Exchequer, and John Davies. Only a few key staff were to move to Coventry.

Barber was clearly astonished by Herberts' decision. He had been under the impression that Churchills was a quite successful company having won the Queen's Award and expanded capacity quite recently. He said that he knew that the firm had experienced certain difficulties but he had thought it was now progressing well. He pleaded with Mr Raine, the managing director of the Herbert Group, a consultant who had been recently brought in to reorganise the group, to review his decision, arguing that the machine tool industry was strongly cyclical and had been suffering from the restrictive economic policies of recent years. But demand was now rising following the Government's new expansionary policy (£1.4 million reduction in taxes, £0.7 million increase in expenditure), although machine tools, being largely required for new plant, tended to lag behind other parts of the economy. Recently, it was true that the total domestic population of machine tools had been declining while world production had increased by 13% since 1970. UK imports of grinding machines had risen from £5.6 million in 1969 to £7.6 million in 1971.

44. A corner of the vast abandoned Churchills' plant – in 1995.

Barber asked Raine to suspend the closure of Churchills if productivity at Broadheath was increased in the following year at least to the level of the Coventry plant. Raine responded that the Broadheath plant had been losing money at about the rate of 10% of sales value over the last three years, over £800,000 losses in all. At no stage did Herberts say that they had given any warning of any need to increase productivity or to reduce losses.

The trade unions advanced other arguments. They said that all machine tool companies had been losing money recently, including Herberts' other plants, because of the national economic situation. The only hope for the maintenance of the engineering industry in Britain was a flourishing machine tool industry. Many engineering workshops in the country had poor or outdated machine tools. Churchills was a good technical company, by no means a lame duck. When Lord Levenshulme had presented the Queen's Award two years previously he had commended the firm for, among other things, increasing exports 120% in three years, with 55% of the production then being exported. They were possibly the largest grinding machine tool producers in Britain. Hardly any UK engineering factory was without Churchill machines, or any country in the world. The company's sales were increasing to the rate of £4 million per annum in late 1971, when the sales of other companies were at their lowest ebb.

During the following months the local *Guardian* was full of stories of industrial trouble. There were power shortages because of the coal strike, many firms were on short time with Churchills down to 60% capacity. Budenbergs had their own electric generator and were working at 80% capacity. 300 men were on strike at Tilghmans over six redundancies. There was a national pay dispute with 2,000 people locked out in the area – the unions saying they were trying to keep up with rising prices and to reduce overtime because of heavy unemployment.

In the midst of all this, Herberts' announced in February that they were deferring the Churchill closure for six months, partly because there were to be joint discussions with the Government about the problems of the machine tool industry in general and Herberts' in particular. But in March they sacked 120 men from the Broadheath plant and there were redundancies at their other factories.

Finally, in June 1972, it was unexpectedly announced that the unions had accepted that the closure of Churchills would go ahead, probably being completed by July 1973. Herberts had lost £4 million in the last financial year after a near break-even the year before.

It is very evident that Churchills were a victim partly of the national economic situation as it was affecting the machine tool industry with particular reference to the restrictive Government measures of recent years. More importantly, they suffered because they were just one member of a group with more deep-seated problems and much vacant capacity. After all, Herberts losses of £4 million in 1971 were of a different order to the alleged £0.3 million loss of Churchills. Herberts seem to have made no attempt to mobilise the local feelings and capabilities of the Churchills staff and workforce to restore profitability. Clearly they had bigger fish to fry in maintaining their own Coventry plant which was in a far worse situation than the Broadheath factory.

There was a significant new development at the beginning of the 1970s in the affairs of another company which had been originally taken over much earlier. J W Record, the founder and owner of Record Electrical, had in 1943 decided to sell his shares to the British Shareholders Trust, a City of London Issuing House, in order to make way for his retirement after the war. In 1955 this Trust was itself taken over by a larger issuing house, i.e. Philip Hill, which was then associated with Elliot Bros. of London. Rather than join the latter, however, the executive directors of Record elected to continue alone and money was raised for this purpose.

The British Shareholders Trust would not agree to this course and suggested that Record should get together with another instrument making company. The only suitable company was Evershed and Vignoles Ltd, a principal competitor, who raised a loan to take over Record. Although the two companies were legally merged, they operated separately and Record Electrical continued to expand, adding a third floor in 1958.

In 1963 the British America Tobacco Company Ltd bought a major interest in Evershed and Vignoles Ltd as a diversification venture into a field away from its normal operation, but it soon became apparent that this type of diversification was not in the best interests of BAT. A merger was therefore sought for Evershed with another instrument-maker which eventually led to a take-over by George Kent in 1966. Finally, in 1971, Record Electrical were taken over by Thorn.

It really seems remarkable that this saga of take-overs should have been the context in which Record Electrical were as successful as they were. Clearly, there was an inner strength which kept them going well for many decades. Yet it seems that there was not as much investment in developing and improving products as there should have been in order to stay abreast of growing competition especially from Germany and Japan. Even the office accommodation was reported in 1968 as 'appalling' after a 1966 project to build an extension to cater for expansion of office and production facilities had been turned down by the new parent company.

It seems clear enough also that Thorns milked Record of its substantial profits in the 1970s in order to bolster their own business in Dover. Thus the scene was set for the more tragic developments of the 1980s.

Perusal of the local *Guardian* newspaper reveals a new feeling of uncertainty and concern towards the mid-1970s, reflecting the difficult national economic situation. In July 1975 a Trafford Council Report declared that industry in Broadheath was finely balanced between decline and revitalisation. There was a larger proportion of under used buildings and vacant sites than in any other part of Trafford. More than 7 acres of land were vacant, and the major problem was the Churchill site. Some modern factories had been built but future expansion was inhibited by bad road access plus the limitations imposed by the proximity of the canal. The importance of a south-western bypass scheme was stressed as was the need for a road connection to the west end of Atlantic Street. The newspaper concluded that it was a picture of an estate which had suffered factory closures in the past but was far from flooded with warehousing to the exclusion of high quality manufacturing.

There were other signs of strain. Tilghman-Wheelabrator had locked out 350 workers over a pay claim for a 25% increase. There were spaces in the Lyon Industrial estate which had taken over the Churchill plant and the council planning committee favoured light industry rather than warehousing.

A conference in January 1976 was told that "our position might not be as bad as others" but in recent years the male labour force had fallen from 6,000 to 4,000. Only three or four factories had order books for four months ahead. The Trades Council called for the supply of stock machines from the Government to provide employment, and for the control of imports and of the export of capital. There was a world recession but inflation and unemployment were worst in the UK.

In March 1976 there were strikes involving sixty people at Dowding and Mills (Northern) Ltd, over four redundancies, and at Record Electrical over the issue of equal pay.

In July 1976 at a meeting with the local MP Fergus Montgomery, representatives of the estate companies and the Council examined the grim prospects for engineering apprenticeships which had suffered a gradual decline since 1970. The engineering section at South Trafford College had contracted so that its current 250 places were less than half the 1969 total, and some courses had been moved to North Trafford College to be close to Trafford Park. It was argued that although engineering was not quite the safe and secure career it was in the 1960s, Broadheath was not going to be in the doldrums forever. So all companies were urged to take on a few more apprentices.

In the same month a press report commented upon the shortage of manufacturing orders. Some firms were recovering but were simply using up stocks of finished or partly manufactured items. One commentator argued that the estate had been in decline for ten to fifteen years with jobs down to a third of the 1960 figure. But this would appear to have been an over-statement of the decline. In March 1977 another report said that jobs had fallen to 4,000 in ten years from a peak of 10,000. A further report said that the Seamons Moss Community Centre was in trouble for lack of support, another sign of the times.

Despite the prevailing gloom which no doubt reflected reductions in business for many Broadheath companies, only one additional firm of significance appeared to be threatened with closure – Scraggs Ltd, manufacturers of textile machinery, who occupied the large factory at the westernmost end of the estate originally the premises of Switchgear and Cowans. With the continuing decline of the British textile trade it was not surprising that the machinery business was in difficulty and in August 1976 the Government announced a £20 million aid scheme for the textile businesses. Certainly Scraggs' problems were continuously in the news in the latter half of 1976 and until they effectively closed in March 1977, although 30 out of 200 workers were retained while the management considered going into the motor cycle business.

During the Scraggs' decline there was more than one reference to the need to avoid a repeat of the Churchills' disaster. A trade union official complained that the closure of Churchills brought an end to the manufacture of heavy grinding machines with hardly any being successfully made at Coventry, a judgement which seems to have been only slightly exaggerated. In November 1976 concern was expressed at the low standard of applicants for engineering apprenticeships which was connected to a lack of confidence in part attributed to the closure of Churchills. Of course this comment could be taken as reflecting a change of emphasis in the sense that there was a demand for apprentices which was not being properly met.

There were other signs of a new ambivalence about the general industrial scene. It was, for instance, said in October 1976 that at Stockport there was a waiting list of firms for industrial sites, but few wanted to go to Broadheath. Yet two developers were said to be constructing two industrial buildings at Broadheath on a speculative basis, despite the fact that half a million square feet of space was vacant.

In this period repeated reference was made to the environmental disadvantage of the Broadheath estate, both because of the access problem and also the general appearance of the area. What had been exceptional siting advantages in the beginning seemed to have become drawbacks. Amongst the scene of substantial success – and some failures – of individual enterprises, there was somehow lacking an effective collective will to improve the condition of the estate as a whole. We can recall the complaint at the height of the 1960s' boom about the dreadful state of the local roads – 2 foot deep potholes on Davenport Lane. Reports of meetings with the MP and Trafford Council in the mid-1970s convey a desperate impression of helplessness, a complete lack of the will to do anything effective to put the local house in order, epitomised in particular in the pathetic failures to provide good local roads and, above all, a western access road to a bypass.

Nevertheless, despite the lack of local collective or municipal effort to improve the Broadheath scene, the ambivalence of 1976 turned very shortly into greater confidence in 1977. Tilghman-Wheelabrator, for instance, who in March suffered a strike of 150 out of their 500 employees, in May were boasting of big orders of dust collection and fume control equipment. Gunn JCB Ltd (said to have been in Broadheath for twenty years and employing sixty people) won orders from the CEGB for three four-wheel driver loaders. There was a Broadheath Recovery Campaign which expressed hopes of the estate continuing to flourish. No longer were reports of industrial difficulties dominating the front page of the local newspaper.

In January 1978 there was talk of the possibility of European Community aid, perhaps to enable a western bypass and access road to be constructed, but this seemed to come to nothing. In October there was talk of Broadheath or Trafford Park becoming the site of a new microprocessing plant costing £50 million and providing up to 4,000 jobs but nothing seemed to come of this either.

Yet in November 1978 the local *Guardian* painted a bright picture of an expanding Broadheath – "the days of gloom and despondency are over". The main problem was now a shortage of skilled workers Geoffrey Budenberg, managing director of the family firm was confident that a good time was in prospect – the company was building a new factory using ultra-modern computers. He had toured the estate and observed extensions being built on some factories as well as new factories and workshops being constructed. The scene was one of urgency and drive. Frank Roberts of Silward Electric Company echoed Budenberg's views.

Despite the environmental problems – epitomised in the jibe about 6,000 people employed in a cul-de-sac – Broadheath had apparently shaken off the traumas of the mid-1970s and the loss of several major original companies. Many newer, smaller firms were doing quite well. With good management, both of industry and the national economy, decades of fruitful operation could yet be foreseen. What actually followed could not.

IX
MONETARISM

The present writer vividly remembers walking into his business office – concerned essentially with export business – the morning after the first budget following the Conservative election victory in 1979. Large reductions in personal income tax were to be offset by an increase in VAT from 8% to 15% and interest rates were sharply raised. The Conservatives had long argued before the 1979 election that all the hassle about control of specific wage increases was unnecessary because control of money supply was sufficient. So taking the budget changes together with the Government's 'laissez-faire' policy on pay increases, it seemed quite clear to me that the country was heading for a swift increase in the general price level from the 10% inflation rate of early 1979. Given the Government's refusal to use any direct controls, it would therefore be necessary to apply savage restrictions on the money supply linked with large increases in interest rates. This in turn would raise the value of sterling. All these factors, high price inflation and wage increases, much higher interest rates, plus a rise in sterling, would inevitably mean disaster for British industry and unbelievable levels of unemployment.

So, when I arrived at the office that morning I said to anyone within earshot that by mid-1980 we would have 20% price inflation and two million unemployed and that we had better start considering now how to run our businesses with costs rising far more quickly than in other countries while sterling, instead of depreciating, which would have been the natural concomitant, would rise rapidly. My forecasts were correct within a few months for 20% price inflation and two million unemployed, and the basic interest rate was at 17%. I do not take any particular credit for an astute appraisal – it seemed all so obvious to me. If it was not obvious to the Government, one has to believe in an astonishing incompetence. All that followed after 1980 was conditioned by the terrible errors of 1979. If the exchange rate of sterling is raised by 35% in a year or so and internal costs rise in the same period by 10-15% more than those in our competitor countries, the effect on British manufacturers who are substantially concerned with exporting, or competing with imports, is the same as if they had to pay a tax of some 50% on the prices of their products. So it was no wonder at all that vast sections of British industry went to the wall.

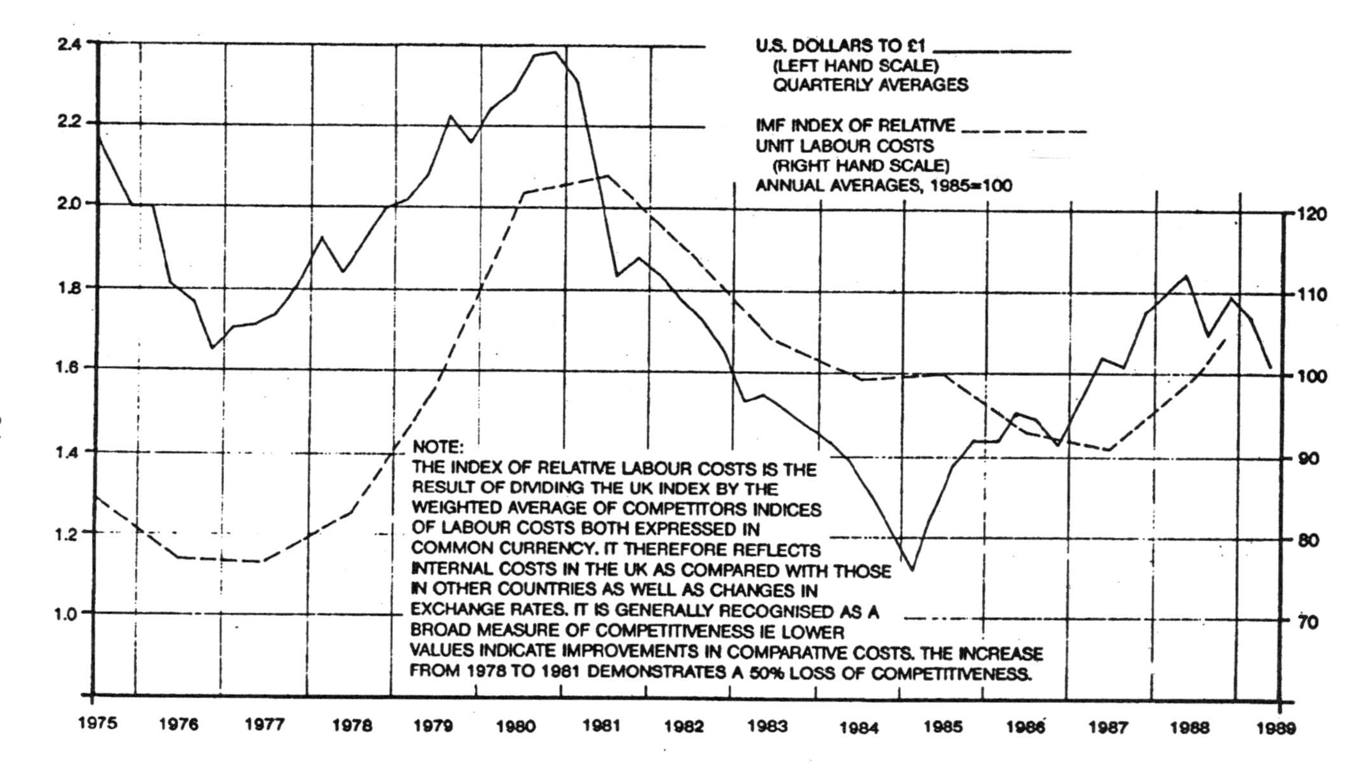

45. *Figure: Exchange value of sterling and manufacturing competitiveness 1975-1989.*

The Government, having deliberately taken the measures contributing to this situation, continued ostentatiously to wash its hands of the consequences, blaming them on market forces, North Sea Oil and so on. The horror of inflation has for many years since then been the bogeyman against which Government policy has been directed. The vehemence of the denunciations against inflation appears to have been partly inspired by the need to conceal that 22% inflation in 1980 was, to a substantial extent, the result of Government policies. In practice, of course, the subsequent years saw the application of monetarist policies designed to bring down the rate of price inflation. But general deflationary measures of this kind constitute a very blunt weapon to reduce price inflation from over 20% to an acceptable 4 or 5%. This is particularly so if an over-strong pound is not only accepted but even welcomed because it keeps down import prices.

It is of course true that in 1979 to 1981 the rise in world oil prices was pushing up the general price level and was also tending to raise the value of sterling. But in these circumstances, the task of Government was to moderate these changes, not to exacerbate them.

To understand something of the impact on British industry of the nightmare economics of 1979-80 it is instructive to read Sir Michael Edwardes' book *Back from the Brink,* which tells the story of his efforts to rescue British Leyland following his appointment by the Callaghan government. The British motor industry is inevitably exposed to the maximum extent to changes in the exchange rate coupled with the general price and cost level in the UK compared to other countries. British Leyland had to compete with foreign car makers over the whole range of its sales both at home and abroad.

By 1979 Edwardes had drawn up his basic plan for reorganising and re-equipping British Leyland, a project which was going to require additional Government funding of some half a billion pounds. As sterling rose higher and higher during 1979 and 1980, Edwardes realised that his original plan was no longer viable. It was necessary to reduce more drastically still the level of operation for British Leyland and at the same time to double the funding required from the Government. Edwardes vividly describes his strenuous effects to persuade the Government and the Bank of England to change their economic policies but if anyone listened, no one would budge an inch.

It was in November 1980 that Edwardes made his famous speech to the CBI in Brighton when he stressed again that the pound was over-

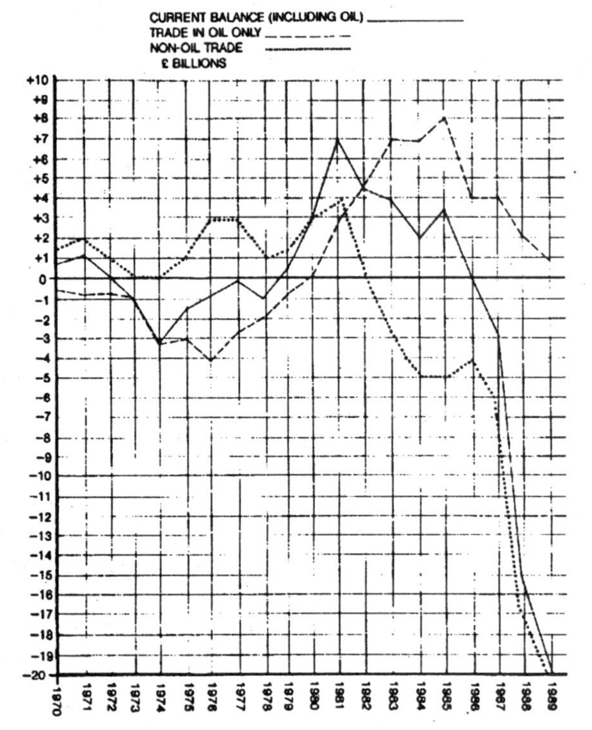

46. Figure: Contribution of trade in oil to balance of payments 1970-1989.

valued, interest rates were penurious and the whole issue was being aggravated by North Sea Oil. At this point came the oft-quoted (and misquoted) remark to the effect that if the Government did not have the wit and the imagination to reconcile our industrial needs with the fact of North Sea Oil, they would do better to "leave the bloody stuff in the ground".

In fact, as Edwardes himself makes clear, it should have been possible to have our cake and eat it. The rate of exploitation of oil should have been controlled as part of a general policy of keeping interest rates and the exchange rate at levels which enabled British industry to be competitive. In this situation, for the Government to argue about leaving everything to market forces was quite pathetic.

So what happened to British industry after the Government's policies of 1979-81? In all the principal sectors of trade, export surpluses, or balances between exports and imports, changed to import excesses in the 1980s with the chemical industry exceptionally maintaining a modest surplus and aerospace equipment increasing its surplus based on the vast Saudi Arabian purchase of military aircraft.

In relation to machine tools, a 1987 report on the kitchen furniture industries in Britain and West Germany found a productivity gap in favour of the latter of 50-60%. Typically, the higher-quality goods were imported into Britain, mainly from Germany. The heavy machinery used in Britain was entirely imported, mainly from Germany and Italy. Automation and machinery was much more effectively used in Germany where production planning and timetabling was much more thoroughly done by highly experienced personnel. The following passage from the conclusions of this report needs to be quoted in full.

> "The net effect of these technological and organisational differences was that the typical German and typical British firms visited were of visibly different calibre. Both had access on international markets to the same selection of modern machinery (i.e. machine tools) but the qualifications of those employed were entirely different. 90% of all German employees had vocational qualifications based on a three year apprenticeship type course followed by qualifying examinations; in Britain only 10% came near to being in that category ... It was with the help of a thoroughly qualified workforce that advanced machinery and operation methods were put into smooth operation and fully exploited. Our YTS scheme caters for an immense number of trainees, but the initial educational qualifications of the trainees and the vocational standards aimed for under the scheme are much below those current in Germany..."

For manufacturing industry as a whole, the total output index fell by 15% between 1979 and 1981-1982. Gross fixed investment in industry fell from £7.5 billion in 1979 to £4.7 billion in 1982. Output did not recover its 1979 level until 1987, and gross fixed investment until 1988.

The trade position for manufactured goods continued to deteriorate through the 1980s as the home economy recovered with industry severely damaged by the trauma of 1979-82. An export surplus of £4.5 billion in 1981 declined to a deficit of over £1.7 billion in 1989. The volume of imports of goods more than doubled from 1978-89 while the volume of exports increased by 30%.

The pound sterling, having risen from $1.85 in mid-1978 to nearly $2.4 late in 1980 fell to $1.10 in 1985 and was back up to $1.85 early in 1988. Clearly this was an extremely turbulent period for everyone involved in industry whether trying to export or competing against imports. Late in the decade came the decision to join the European Monetary System at an unsustainably high level in 1990, a policy which collapsed in the autumn of 1992. This high level again caused serious trade problems and was associated with the recession from 1989 which followed the supposed 'economic miracle' brought about by reduced

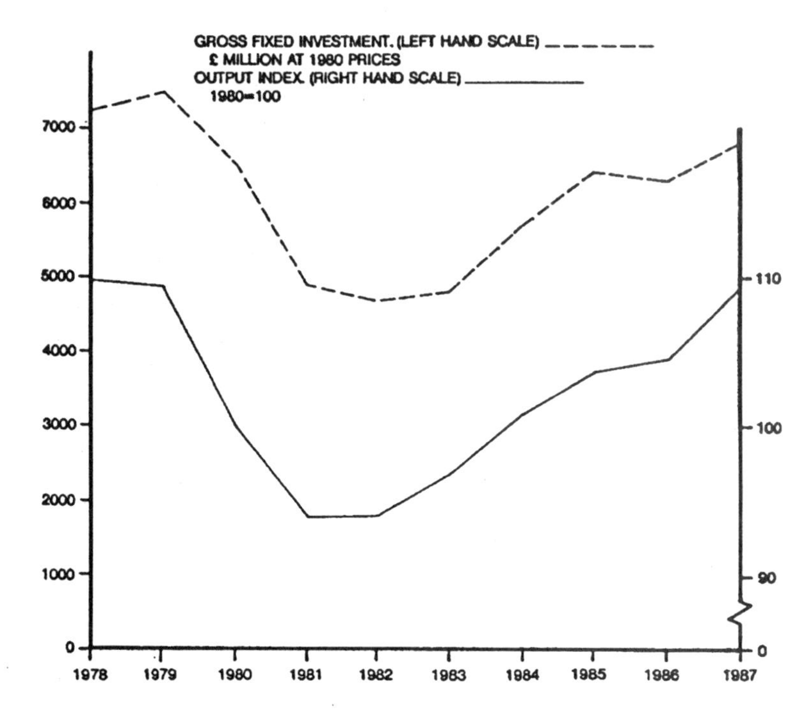

47. Figure: Investment and output in manufacturing industry 1978-1987.

taxation for well-to-do people and a great credit expansion all too reminiscent of the Barber boom of the early 1960s.

Now in 1995 we have sterling at a sensible level and a modest economic revival which is stalling with industrial investment still far too low. A new report on World Competitiveness by independent international organisations in September 1995 said that Britain's overall standing had fallen in a year from fourteenth to eighteenth. For the strength of the manufacturing base, Britain was in thirty-fifth place, for the teaching of science and technology in school thirty-ninth and for the availability of qualified engineers fortieth.

X
THE TRAGEDIES OF THE 1980S IN BROADHEATH

In the early months of 1980 the *Altrincham Guardian* ran a series of articles on the Broadheath estate and some of its chief companies. The general message was that times were difficult; there was a slump even – and that Broadheath's decline was the result of the nation's economic slide. In this situation, the local manufacturing dinosaurs were "virtually extinct" – a touch exaggerated perhaps since Kearns-Richards, Tilghmans and Record Electrical all insisted they were facing the future with cautious optimism – in the sense that in these deteriorating times, their effect on unemployment would be negligible. It was reported that 4,200 to 4,500 people were employed on the estate compared with 6,000 to 8,000 in its heyday – all these figures appear to be on the low side. (In fact the 1981 Census shows 4,650 people employed in industry in Broadheath, plus 740 in warehousing and distribution and 350 in offices and this was after many jobs had been lost early in 1981.)

In the meantime a new generation of small-scale pioneers had appeared in businesses such as scientific instruments, medical equipment, computer systems and a wide range of electronic components, many of them in the estate's newest development site off Dairyhouse Lane. Atlantic Street had been extended into the countryside in the 1970s but few new jobs had been created. A number of vacated premises had been converted for light industry, warehousing and storage. Once again there were complaints about a shortage of skilled engineers as a result of the steep decline in apprenticeships. Most companies were said to be fairly busy.

Clearly it was again a time of uncertainty – "Is the area's industrial future as bumpy and pothole-strewn as Atlantic Street?"

A list was given of the firms which had disappeared from Broadheath over the years:

1939	Thornton-Pickard
1968	Switchgear and Cowans (whose building was taken over by Scraggs)
1972	Churchills, with the loss of 1,200 jobs

1972	MSU – specialised machines for Rolls Royce Aerospace Division
1978	Scraggs textile machinery
1978	J B Hyde trading machine makers
1978	Clare Colletts – had wound up their manufacturing operation making a patent range of milling equipment

The *Guardian* reported on some individual operating companies.

Kearns-Richards

There had been severe problems following Richards' merger with Kearns in 1967 (as a division of Staveleys) because of technical incompatibilities. Large scale redundancies had followed and Richards' foundry had closed. Only in recent years had Kearns-Richards regained something of their former market pre-eminence. They were making twice as many units as in 1967, had a good export standing and were profitable. Their machines, costing £15,000 to £250,000, were used throughout industry to produce valves, pumps and gear-boxes for a wide range of uses, with 35% going for export.

According to Mr Styles, their managing director, the future would be no easier but should not be markedly worse. The silicon chip was adding a new dimension to their machines.

From other evidence it seems clear that with little left of the Richards' range of machines by the late 1970s, the company had established a new identity of products derived mainly from the Kearns' technology. It was, however, falling behind the Japanese, in particular, in introducing computer controlled machines.

Linotype

This company's dominant position in the printing machinery business had been lost because of successive technological advances. Thus the Linotype Company was always struggling from the 1950s onwards. In that decade eight machines a week were produced at Broadheath, falling to five or six in the 1960s. They had moved into book printing and binding in the early 1970s.

What the *Guardian* article did not report was that the parent company had closed its three other factories in other countries, since the demand for their products had fallen to a low level, and concentrated production at Broadheath. The number of employees there had fallen from 1,800 in the 1960s to 750 by early 1980, another forty having recently been discharged. By late 1980 the parent company had lost confidence in the Broadheath operation whose problems were greatly exacerbated by the British recession and the high value of sterling, and were unwilling to invest further in its technology. Thus the reduction of operations by almost half in 1981, which is reported below, was intended to lead to complete closure.

Tilghmans

Since 1972 this company had been a wholly-owned subsidiary of the American Wheelabrator Company, from which it had taken a licence in the mid-1930s for the production of airless shot-blast machines. In early 1980, 450 people were employed at Broadheath by Tilghman-Wheelabrator as the company was now called, but in September eighty redundancies were declared.

From other sources it is clear that Tilghmans, after benefiting greatly from heavy involvement in war production up to 1945 had developed in the post-war economic period better than most Broadheath companies. However, most of their machines were destined for foundries, the numbers of which declined in the UK over the whole period. They had been taken over by Staveleys in 1951 along with Richards which they owned, but Staveleys really wanted the latter because of its machine tool business. Staveleys had therefore gradually moved away from the Tilghman business and it became a separate company before being taken over by Wheelabrator. The latter owned plants in several other countries and controlled their markets so that the Broadheath company could sell overseas only to Scandinavia, Eastern Europe and the former British Empire countries.

Budenbergs

This company was another of the 'originals' and the only one to survive as a family concern. In the Second World War they had made pressure gauges for submarines and in 1980 were helping to equip nuclear submarines, power stations, sewage and water plants and oil and chemical factories, particularly with pressure testing equipment. They claimed to have fared better than most in the 'slump'. Recently they had built a new factory of 26,000 square feet in Craven Road on land taken over from Tilghmans, as there was plenty of demand for factory units and not many vacant sites; further, the company wished to have a separate plant for the production of dead-weight testers which it wanted to put under its own works manager. When the company started at Broadheath in 1914 they employed 114 people and early in 1980 the number was 470.

Castleton Steam Packing

This company, which had operated at Broadheath since 1904, had always specialised in special gland packings for steam locomotives, but had extended into conveyor belting. Thomas Anderson who had acquired Castletons in 1946, ten years later launched Atlantic Rubber Company to make new products including waterproof membranes. Altogether, forty people were employed in 1980.

Record Electrical

This company, which had in 1951 moved into the graphic recorder market, had in 1971 been taken over by Thorn Electric and the number of employees was reduced from 600 to 360. The firm was said to be developing positively for the first time in a number of years. Their instruments were widely used in many scientific-type establishments including Jodrell Bank.

Smaller Companies

The *Altrincham Guardian* also reported on a number of small new companies which were participating in the second industrial revolution based on the silicon chip: the V G Instruments Group making mass spectrometers, 70% for export and winning a Queen's Award; Woolley Compressors employing fifty people, AWL Electronics making microprocessors and a new range of digital thermometers with a 75% export rate in less than thirty years; and V G Data Systems who had doubled their turnover from 1974 and employed fifty people.

1981

By the end of 1980 the quite hopeful scene portrayed at the beginning of the year was clouding over badly. The *Guardian* headline for 11 December read 'BROADHEATH BOMBSHELLS' and the paper reported that the situation was the worst in the estate's history. There were warnings of widespread redundancy.

Tilghmans were expecting seventy redundancies, but were experimenting with short-time working as an alternative. Kearns-Richards were working a three-day week and were, nevertheless, calling for seventy-five voluntary redundancies. Budenbergs were in dispute with their employees over forty compulsory redundancies. Record

Electrical said that a three-day week was imminent with redundancies likely in the new year. Linotype gave protective redundancy notices to all their 540 staff, saying that despite a world-wide sales campaign they still had no orders for their new offset printing machines; they were, however, still the biggest employer on the estate.

Early in January members of the Broadheath Joint Committee met MP Fergus Montgomery who arranged to go to see the Chancellor of the Exchequer, Sir Geoffrey Howe. The message was that the estate's struggle for survival stemmed from the high pound, trade barriers and subsidies overseas, and failure in other countries to meet health and safety rules and other regulations. Also mentioned was the Government's withdrawal of Intermediate Area Status in favour of Enterprise Zones including Trafford Park.

On 22 January the local newspaper reported that 500 jobs had been lost in six days – the worst news since the closure of Churchills in the early 1970s. Record Electrical had sacked ninety-two because of the 'economic recessions'. Linotype, following their warning in December, dismissed 240 employees, 45% of all levels, blaming mainly the high exchange rate of sterling against the dollar. Barry-Wehrmiller Ltd, makers of the bottle washing plant for breweries, dairies and soft drink manufacturers, who had opened in the former Scraggs factory only the previous year, chopped 180 out of 240 jobs and abandoned the major part of their product range, blaming the high level of the pound; 70% of their sales had been for export in competitive markets.

By the end of January, unemployment in Altrincham and Sale exceeded 3,000, a post-war record, with at least 500 more expected shortly. The number of executive and professional people without jobs had risen by over 100 in one year.

It was not that Broadheath companies were not making strenuous efforts to maintain their businesses. In February Kearns-Richards announced orders worth £¾ million for their large horizontal boring and smelting machines from a Gateshead marine engineering company and the USA, with smaller machines with sophisticated computer controls going to India for £200,000. The company had been on a three-day week since October and although by strenuous marketing they were securing some overseas orders were finding the home demand very poor. Basically, their failure to keep up with development of computer control was their undoing. In 1979 they had been selling over eighty machines of their popular smaller type – the SH75 – but by 1984 only three were sold in the year.

In March 1981, Luke and Spencer, one of the early estate firms making grinding and cutting wheels, announced it was to close in May with the loss of 185 jobs. The decision had been taken by their parent company, Unicorn Industries Ltd of Stafford, because of low orders, attributable to the high exchange rate, more competition from abroad and the severe economic recession. Luke and Spencer's wheels had been used by British Rail for smoothing tracks as well as extensively in steel works and foundries. They had been on a four-day week since October as a result of orders falling to £2 million year from £5 million four years ago, most shockingly over the last six months. They paid tribute to the good labour relations which they had always enjoyed.

In December 1981 Record Electrical sacked another forty out of 205 remaining employees, saying times were still exceedingly difficult with depressed markets. They were planning to buy-in certain services.

By mid-1985, Record Electrical were in serious difficulties and most of their work was transferred to their parent company's plants in Dover and Leamington Spa. Complete closure of the Broadheath operation was averted by a management buy-out by directors Ron Hembrough and Danny O'Driscoll. Operations were greatly scaled down so that only nineteen people were employed in one-third of the Atlantic Street factory, the rest to be leased to small engineering firms. They were looking for orders from old customers like Rolls Royce and BNFL, and were hopeful of an industrial mortgage.

1982

In February 1982 Barry-Wehrmiller were concerned that the owners of the former Scraggs factory were going to sell it over their heads, but they managed to secure a twenty year lease a quarter of the 120,000 square feet space. They were employing seventy-five people on electronic bottle inspection equipment.

In March 1982, Kearns-Richards were optimistic again, working round the clock on a £7 million order from the USA – a far cry from a year before. They were most anxious to disprove the idea that British firms were unreliable on delivery dates. They still had 320 employees.

Yet in July the wheel had turned again and the company dismissed ninety workers leaving only some 220, blaming the world recession and especially the decline in the US market for machine tools. In October, there was more short-time working as orders were deferred, and in November a further eighty-five redundancies were declared leaving less than sixty people. Machine shop manufacturing came to an end and the company was reduced to the assembly of machines and the provision of spares and services. At least half the Atlantic Street factory was put on the market.

By the end of 1982 unemployment in Altrincham and Sale was well over 5,000.

The whole British machine tool industry was said to be suffering as customers had no money. Kearns-Richards' products were declared to be "right and better developed" than those of competitors, and they had raised their export percentage from thirty to seventy in two years. However, as we have explained, the company did have severe competitive problems in relation to computer control and late in 1983, Staveleys decided to close it down. The managing director, Brian Bottomley, with his son Nigel, an accountant who was not in the company, and Gordon Greenwood, bought out the business for which they were granted a fifteen year mortgage of £414,000 by Trafford Council. A grant of £100,000 came from the Government. They secured two new orders worth £0.5 million but were employing only thirty-five men. Part of their factory was leased to Springfields Tools Machine Com-

48. A corner of the H W Kearns (later Kearns-Richards) building in 1995. The huge production plant has had a modern cladding fitted.

pany in which a former Kearns-Richards sales director, R Lovell, was involved.

In October 1984, prospects for Kearns-Richards appeared brighter than for some years with nine new orders for £1.3 million eight of them for export. Employee numbers were increased to forty-five. They were particularly proud of a £350,000 order for a computer controlled floor borer for a ship-building firm in Virginia, USA. In 1987 they took over a Crewe-based firm Hosan Machine Tool Co, suppliers to the Ministry of Defence and car manufacturers. Twenty-five new jobs took their total to 140 with 1987 turnover rising to over £4 million.

The company made strenuous efforts to develop new products including smaller Kearns-type machines and a large machine derived from an old Richards model, but development periods of three to five years were involved. In the meantime the company had bencome dependant for nearly half their business on sales of lathes to Matrix Churchill. The clamp down on equipment sales to Iraq meant that Kearns-Richards lost their lathes business by the end of 1989 and they were in serious financial difficulty so that the receivers were called in by the banks. The remnants of the company were sold off and the building put up for auction. It was bought by Blue Chip Holdings for £2 million and divided for use by a number of commerical enterprises.

During the early 1980s the vital need was repeatedly stressed for improving access to the estate, but the western bypass had been abandoned. There was, however, a new plan to widen Dairyhouse Lane south from its junction with Hanover Road and for an extension to Atlantic Street, with a view to encouraging the development of 22 acres of land to the north of the railway.

In the meantime the other big older companies were still working hard to maintain their businesses in difficult circumstances.

The remains of the Linotype Company after the 1981 contraction were saved only by one of the earliest management buy-outs on the part of four of its senior staff after negotiations with the parent company lasting two years which involved the change of name to L & M Ltd. Since then the most strenuous management efforts have been made to adopt and develop new technologies as well as to diversify the company's business in the field of printing presses and related operations such as the fabrication of precision sheet metal enclosures for computer presses. Company acquisition and the establishment of agencies have been involved. Business has been sought and obtained in many parts of the world, which is just as well since for the period of nine months to June 1991, no UK orders had been received, so devastating had the latest recession become. The production director described the last twelve months as the worst business year he had experienced in forty years with the company. For a number of years in the 1980s L & M had given employment to 150 people, but the number was down to eighty-five in June 1991.

Budenbergs, who had factories also in Wales and Australia, had survived in essentially the same business of pressure gauge manufacture by progressively using more up-to-date methods, employing less labour.

By 1991 they were down to 200 people at Broadheath, claiming to be the largest makers of precision dead-weight testers in Europe and the largest makers of pressure gauges in Britain, exporting to over forty companies, although much of their exporting is indirect through customer countries. In 1991 the Budenberg family finally sold out because there was no one left in the family willing and able to run the company. It was taken over as a running concern by Burnfields who soon declared seventy people redundant.

Tilghman-Wheelabrator still employed 400 people at Broadheath until 1992 when they decided to transfer production of stationary equipment to their Halifax plant where they believed costs were lower and labour more flexible. Production of Blastrac portable shot blast machines was retained at Broadheath.

Since then the Broadheath operation has otherwise become mainly an office which acts as the European headquarters for Wheelabrator Engineering Systems Inc. which has a total of fourteen facilities in Europe. The mission of Wheelabrator is to be the provider of environmental services which employ innovative technology, maximise material re-use, and engineer solutions to meet the clean air, clean water and solid waste disposal needs of a variety of companies.

Until the move to Halifax, which was accompanied by a change to using many local sub-contractors in specialist areas, the company had traditionally made all its own components. Clearly, until this move took place, Tilghmans were one of the few great survivors of the pre-First World War Broadheath companies who had quite successfully adapted their business to changing technology and declining or more competitive markets.

They had developed a range of smaller machines because of the great run-down of large British engineering companies needing the bigger machines in which Tilghmans had previously specialised. It ap-

49. The Tilghman-Wheelabrator offices and Blastrac plant in 1995.

pears that this was an example of adaptation to changing market conditions which the other part of the original firm – the George Richards company – had failed to follow.

P I Castings, who had had some redundancies in the 1980-1981 period, appeared to have survived the worst of the recession and in 1985 they still had 260 employees. However, in that year the company, which until then was owned by the original four families who no longer wished to continue in the business, was bought out by three working directors. Since then they have diversified considerably. In 1987 they joined with Sheffield Engineers to form Turbotech Precision Products making high quality compressor wheels which cost £1 million to launch. Later they formed AMTAC, a company providing materials testing and consultancy requirements. The original company now heads the ATR Group and continues to make high quality precision investment castings to meet a wide variety of special requirements. The whole group still employs some 200 people in 1995.

They have continuously sought new markets and adapted their products and processes but still in 1995 use the same basic moulding technique. Improved processes enable 120 people in 1995 to make more castings than 300 people in 1970.

Their old sister company, C S Madan, pump manufacturers, after merging with a Croydon company in 1986 and investing in new com-

50. The old Tilghmans No.4 plant – mainly occupied by a steel distributor in 1995.

51. Part of the vast former Tilghmans (earlier Richards) plant destined to make way for a retail warehouse park.

puter controlled machinery, were taken over in 1992 and their work transferred to Romford where twenty out of sixty-eight employees were offered jobs.

Castleton Steam Packing found their engine market progressively disappearing and developed their Atlantic Rubber Company as an alternative. The latter has outlived its parent and continues in 1995 to operate on a small scale, supplying a variety of hoses, belts, sheets, couplings etc.

NEI, who had taken over Baldwin and Francis in the 1970s to make equipment for the mining industries, struggled along as the coal mining industry was largely destroyed, until they closed in 1991.

So it came about that the Broadheath Industrial Estate which had started in 1885, slowly developed over the following eighty years until it employed some 10,000 people at its peak around 1965, had in twenty short years shrunk to a shadow of its former self, employing perhaps 2,000 people. Three of the early ten great companies had disappeared altogether. The remainder, struggling to survive, had shrunk into different forms and shapes and employed less than 1,000 people between them.

52. Davenport Lane 1995. Shows electricity sub-station on left where Altrincham Electric Supply Co. stood. P I Castings can be seen further down on left.

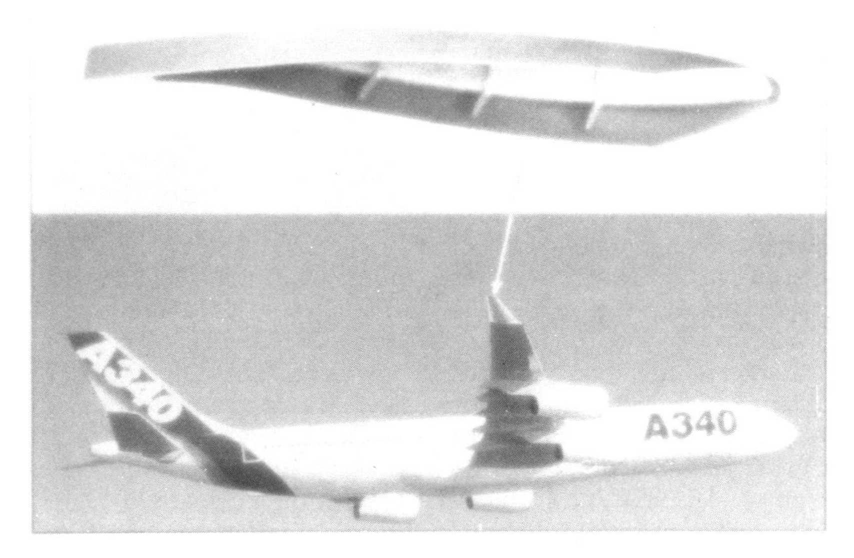

53. P I Castings, aeroplane wing tip in aluminium.

As the 1980s wore on, the estate was being progressively taken over by retail warehouse establishments, distribution organisations and small hi-tech companies dealing in information systems and the like. Of the distributors one of the most notable in 1995 is Gunn JCB handling and servicing JCB construction, materials handling and agricultural machinery.

There is, however, an important manufacturing survivor at the far end of Atlantic Street with sprawling premises occupying several sites totalling 16 acres, including large parts of the major plants most recently owned by NEI and Barry-Wehrmiller – originally Baldwin and Francis and Switchgear and Cowans, before one comes to the newer office buildings. This is Cartwrights who make mainly van bodies, trailers and semi-trailers but have diversified into metalled products such as demountable systems. It is still a family company founded some thirty-five years ago and employs 310 people, many of them skilled. So there is more than one company at Broadheath which actually makes something! And Cartwrights are the biggest employers in the area.

In the next chapter we shall consider the reasons for the industrial tragedy and the metamorphosis of Broadheath.

XI
CONCLUSIONS

In reflecting on the rise and fall of the Broadheath Industrial Estate we must not overlook certain basic limiting factors. Whilst the estate benefited originally from a favourable location including proximity to a vital canal and to railways and a main road, the difficulty of access to the site, partly arising from the very presence of the canal, clearly became a disadvantage in the age of the motor vehicle. Failure to secure a western access to Atlantic Street became a significant handicap.

Compare this situation with the implications of the opening of another canal in 1894, just after Broadheath had begun to develop. The Manchester Ship Canal, facilitating the transportation of heavy machinery, undoubtedly stimulated the development of the Trafford Park estate at a crucial time. Trafford Park had ample space to develop whereas Broadheath was hemmed in by canal, railway and road. Trafford Park had good access routes of various kinds whereas the only road at Broadheath was the A56. Trafford Park grew to several times the size of Broadheath. But Trafford Park also died. So although there were severe limitations on the growth of Broadheath, not least the very existence of Trafford, we have to look for other reasons for Broadheath's decline and fall.

In any event it must be recognised that Broadheath, with its original advantages, had by the mid-1960s filled out to cover a long length of Atlantic Street and alongside the canal as well as a large area north of the railway. In the age of the road vehicle, this was probably the maximum feasible expansion for industries needing to move quantities of heavy materials and goods, given the access problem.

One of the strangest aspects of the development of the estate was the lack of a communal will to improve both the local and access roads. When the industrial activity was at its height there were frequent complaints about potholes, some of which still seem to remain despite fairly recent improvements to Atlantic Street itself. It also seems odd in retrospect that the two roads between the areas north and south of the railway have remained so poor and narrow.

The great industrial value in the estate should surely have made it worthwhile to improve the local environment and road communications, but it seems that individual enterprise was not matched by a co-operative or communal spirit.

There was also the bigger question of improving access to the whole area by building a link road to the west. Since all the public roads in that area are only country lanes leading nowhere in particular a major new road would have been required – including a western bypass for Altrincham and Sale. Many plans for such a road have been made and abandoned, including two major schemes in the last ten years. However, the justification for these was mainly the relief of the A56, and they would in any case have been too late to save Broadheath.

There were also limits, surely, on effective labour supply. The total population of Altrincham, including Timperley, was a little over 40,000 in the 1960s, men, women and children. So employment approaching 10,000 was extremely high even allowing for other areas when few working men and women had cars. In the 1960s a quarter of all employed people in Altrincham and Sale were working in Broadheath.

Yet there are some other curious and substantial aspects of the nature and rate of development of the estate. The major companies which were to constitute the heart of the area took thirty-five years in all to arrive. Once there they endured, with one significant exception, pretty well up to the peak period after another forty-five years. After 1919 no other major industrial company joined the estate except for two sizeable firms well after the Second World War – Baldwin and Francis and Switchgear and Cowans.

The modest new arrivals of the inter-war years appear not to have survived into the peak years of the 1960s.

It is therefore without surprise that we note that most of the major Broadheath companies fall into two groups both arising from the essential requirements of manufacturing industry in the post-textile age – machine tools and measuring instruments. Printing machinery (Linotype) was also a basic requirement of the new expanding world of industry and knowledge.

At no time did Broadheath have any significant representatives of the principal twentieth century industries of motor cars, chemicals or glass, although there were one or two modest companies on the fringe of electrical engineering. It is of course possible to argue that in the economically disturbed inter-war period when these industries were being developed behind tariff walls, there was such concentration and cartelisation elsewhere that there was no realistic opportunity for Broadheath to participate in them. In any event the economic situation in the inter-war years was so difficult until the later 1930s that it is perhaps not so surprising that new major entrants to the estate did not arrive. On the other hand, the old established firms did survive, aside from Thornton-Pickard which had had managerial and financial problems for a long time and whose life was perhaps prolonged by the First World War, which no doubt helped other Broadheath companies.

So also did the 1939-45 war which was followed by a prolonged, if at times unsteady, period of economic expansion. The long-established companies continued to flourish until, in the case of Richards and later Kearns, they were taken over by companies who were strangers to the machine tool business. Most of the new companies which arrived during the 1950s reflected a new and somewhat more affluent age – they were rather like froth on the serious business of machine tools, precision machining and measuring operations.

The first serious hiccough in the post-war prosperity occurred in the mid-1970s when the national economy was in the grip of the considerable disturbances of the miners' strike, the three-day week and the huge increase in oil prices, stimulating roaring inflation. As the national economy settled down to a modest recovery in the late 1970s, so did the Broadheath estate – except, that is, for Churchills, the prosperous company which had succumbed to take-overs by incompetent people looking for orders and perished, leaving the huge scar of vast empty buildings on the estate.

Churchills, like Richards, Tilghmans and Linotype, had strong American origins or connections. Budenbergs were German. Only Kearns, Luke and Spencer, Thornton-Pickard and Record Electrical and a few lesser concerns were indisputably British. It is difficult to understand the extent of the foreign involvement. It may have in part been coincidence or personal or national contacts. There was a direct connection between Richards and Tilghmans who were joined together in business from the early days. But it is hard to resist some implication that it was a reflection of the growing superiority of American and German technology over British. Possibly the durability of these companies had a little to do with their foreign ownership and top management, although in the case of Linotype the American ownership and direction, involving the milking of profits, was of doubtful benefit and it was strong British management which pulled the company together in the 1960s. Certainly Thornton-Pickard seem to have been a classic example of British lack of ability to exploit promising inventions.

Now it might be said that the very fact that most of these companies had been around for the best part of a century, often in several generations of family ownership, might suggest that their business practices and technologies were out-of-date in the modern and increasingly electronic world of international competition and that their future potential was very limited.

There may be some truth in this proposition but it was not an inevitable consequence. Of course there has always been the risk that successive generations of the same family are not as able or dynamic as the founder. Death duties may have eaten into capital. Perhaps the greatest risk has been that in a highly technological field inadequate resources have been available for investing in research and development to keep abreast of competitors. Without the same kind of close banking support as in Germany, for instance, the only way of raising capital would be by selling shares. This way control could well be lost.

Certainly some of the big Broadheath companies had been taken over by the 1960s. Asset stripping appears not to have been a motive, but in some cases the acquisition of orders clearly was. One result of a take-over was certain, i.e. that local loyalties were diluted. The spirit of a family company embedded in the local community tended to be lost. When business became difficult in another area or plant, a Broadheath factory could be sacrificed without concern about the consequences in its local area.

Record Electrical appear to have drifted somewhat through various ownership changes until they were taken over by Thorn and were said by 1980 to be positively managed but their profiles were being milked and development neglected until in 1981 disaster struck a near-fatal blow in the shape of national economic policy. Luke and Spencer had also been taken over in the early 1970s by Unicorn Industries of Stafford but seemed to be in reasonably good shape in 1980. In 1981 they perished.

The extent of take-overs of Broadheath companies is by no means untypical of British industry. Indeed it is by way of being a pecularly British disease, although not very different from the situation in the USA. The ease with which unsolicited and 'hostile' take-overs can be achieved gives rise to an unduly short-term attitude to profits and share prices, to the detriment of long-term investment. The German system is quite different with hostile take-overs being very difficult. There the banks are closely involved in industry on a long-term investment basis. If an industrial company gets into difficulty, the bank involved will be concerned to help it out, ensuring good management and a long-term outlook.

Of course the Broadheath companies were inevitably affected very closely by economic and business conditions in the rest of the country, if only because their customers were involved. But the effect of the take-overs was to put the estate very much at the mercy of the specific business problems of owning companies in other areas. Many Broadheath people, employers and employees alike, had tended to regard their estate as a kind of cosy world of its own, an illusion that was rudely shattered after the peak years of the mid-1960s.

In fact most of the important companies were taken over before 1980, mainly by other British companies but two by Americans – one early, Linotype, and one late, Tilghmans who had earlier also been taken over by Staveleys. So control was lost, in two cases overseas, over manufacturing and sales policy and, above all, over research and development. This is a sobering thought when, for instance, almost the whole 'British' car industry is foreign owned.

Of course, Linotype had been struggling for many years after losing their dominant technical position yet they seemed to be strongly managed and in reasonably optimistic mood through the 1970s, although operating at a reduced level. Like the other estate companies they had valuable assets in the shape of skilled and experienced workers who had loyally served them for many years. Labour relations had almost invariably been good. All the companies were well established and respected in the local community with a long history of good management. Yet 1981 proved to be the last straw for Linotype's American owners.

There was a special problem in the vital machine tools industry. As we have explained, the huge expansion of the textile and railway industries in the middle of the nineteenth century stimulated a vast demand for machinery to make the textile goods and railway engines and equipment and then ships. This in turn created a requirement for the machine tools to make the machinery and the engines. So the modern machine tool industry in Britain was born out of practical necessity. It was carried along further by the newer industries of shipbuilding and motor vehicles.

It was, however, moved along on a very down-to-earth and practical basis. Real current problems, the need for more accurate and flexible tools, the demand for tools for new processes, were generally met as they arose. Nobody devoted research and development to inventing more sophisticated tools as a business in itself. Provision for university courses in this kind of applied engineering did not exist. Technical training for staff followed the traditional route of long apprenticeships and evening classes. The most senior staff were very poorly qualified.

For half a century this approach served the British machine tool industry well enough. Two world wars really benefited Kearns and Richards – they produced between them the vast majority of UK military requirements for their vital kind of machine tools – and in between the wars they and Churchills survived the growing competition from Germany and the USA. Even so, there were serious difficulties, even as late as 1936 as indicated by the 1980 press report about orders from Russia.

We have noted the pent-up demand after the Second World War which kept the machine tool firms busy for a number of years, with order books too full to leave much time for concern about future development. By the 1950s, however, there was a growing appreciation that the world was becoming a different place, that international competition required stronger units than the fragmented British industry. The Germans were already seen to be catching up and moving ahead in some parts of the market. An industrial review report encouraged the idea of mergers and take-overs in the UK. It could be said that it was in this context that the Alfred Herbert Company took over BSA Tools and Churchills, but Herberts were already in trouble. Staveleys' take-over of first Richards and then Kearns could be regarded as being in the same category, although Staveleys had a special position because their main business had been nationalised and they were not really in machine tools.

In any event, these mergers did not necessarily provide more robust units without adequate attention to the need for a strong technical base and large research and development expenditure. The machine tool industry was by no means alone in Britain in its failure to invest enough on a long-term basis. This certainly appears to have been true of Richards after being taken over by Staveleys in 1951.

By 1975 Germany dominated the sale of machine tools in Europe. Japan soon acquired the world leadership by their typical method of government-led creation of technology and capacity, first to copy and then to overhaul foreign suppliers behind doors closed to further imports. In many industries the very machinery to make goods in Britain was by the 1980s typically imported. A 1987 report on timber and wooden furniture showed the heavy machinery coming mainly from Germany and Italy.

So by the time Staveleys took over H W Kearns in 1967 they were already losing money on their machine tool company acquisitions including Richards. Presumably the profitable and technologically-advanced H W Kearns was attractive to them. But they put in charge of the joint Kearns-Richards operation a man who had no knowledge of machine tools and made many of the Kearns' commercial and development staff redundant.

Although by 1980 Kearns-Richards had made strenuous efforts to consolidate and improve their business and still employed some 400 people, like other British companies they were falling behind in respect of computer application.

The demise of Churchills merits special mention. Whatever the original motives of Alfred Herbert in acquiring the company, as part of the BSA Group, there is doubt that the closure of Churchills was a cynical move of desperation. There appears to have been no prior warning, no evident effort to mobilise the staff to achieve better results. Indeed with the very recent accolade of Queen's Awards, the company might have been excused a degree of self-satisfaction. Cynical may seem a harsh word, but how else does one describe the sudden decision to discard over a thousand people, without warning or the chance to save themselves, wrecking the lives of so many families and severely damaging the industrial estate and the local economy?

The paternalism of the original Broadheath companies in the tradition of family businesses was being abandoned in favour of the heartless handling of human beings as if they were just factors of production like supplies of materials to be cut off with a ruthless stroke of the pen by other companies with self-inflicted problems.

Of course, it may well be that the Broadheath companies as a whole, many of them taken over, despite the optimistic notes of the press reports in 1979 and 1980, were reasonably typical of much of British industry in not being in the most healthy of conditions to withstand further major economic shocks. It would, after all, have been surprising if they were, given the general British social aversion to industry, the dire neglect of technological education and training, the lack of long-term banking support, and the exposed position of the British economy to international trade and financial fluctuations precipitating the stop-go government policies of the 1960s and 1970s, which so discouraged investment. Yet some of the larger companies had striven hard to keep up with technical change and had together created a technological community by no means to be despised.

Against this background, clearly what was needed was a set of policies to remedy these long-running defects, to encourage new industrial investment and to strengthen manufacturing as the heart of the British economy, so that a hand-to-mouth existence could be made a thing of the past. The advent of the national fortune of North Sea Oil afforded the opportunity for such a policy. Instead, what Broadheath, Trafford Park and the rest of British industry suffered was the crippling policies of 1979-1981 which coupled rampant inflation with a swift increase in the value of sterling.

The resulting damage was lethal or near-lethal to Linotype, Luke and Spencer, Kearns-Richards and Record Electrical. To Budenbergs, Tilghman-Wheelabrator and the others it was certainly damaging. Even if a company survives this kind of unprecedented attack, its future must inevitably be prejudiced by its loss of skilled people and of the financial resources for investment in the future, quite apart from the loss of market share for companies whether in exports or in competing against imports.

Sir John Harvey-Jones ('Troubleshooter'), who was Chairman of ICI in the early 1980s, declared that he had lost a third of his UK customers in manufacturing industry within a few years. Some of the politicians and economists who were responsible for the economic policies which caused this immense damage have claimed, after the event, that they were simply removing a lot of dead wood or museum pieces from the British economy. It is hard to believe that these people really intended to do this and to make 3 or 4 million people unemployed. No, much more likely that it was the unavoidable but quite unforeseen result of applying the dogma of monetarism and the unrestricted market

If these companies had been given the benefit of more stable economic conditions as well as of a modicum of Government support, which the uncovenanted wealth of North Sea Oil could have afforded, they could certainly have survived for many more years by adapting to the changing technical and economic conditions of the late twentieth century. Whatever good purpose was served by destroying them? Was it by any relevant standard necessary to throw so many people on the scrap-heap to be supported by the dwindling number of people with jobs? Would it not have been far better if many of them had had the continuing opportunity to earn their own living for a fair period ahead, even if some of their companies had eventually succumbed to the winds of change?

In Britain, we need to accord a new dignity and importance to making useful things rather than making money in financial markets. We need to remember that human dignity requires that people are, or should be, participants in a working community and deserve to be led and encouraged to do demanding jobs rather than treated as figures in an accounts book. It is hard to believe that in Britain, in 1995, the Government takes credit for opting out, not only of the minimum wage but even the obligation on companies to operate proper arrangements for consultation with their workpeople. After all, Linotype got the latter right a century ago. For many years also, they, like Richards and Tilghmans, operated a system by which their employees shared in profits or cost savings.

Opposition to a minimum wage is in fact consistent with the British failure in respected of technical education and training epitomised in the national backwardness in the application of computers to industry both at the senior management level and on the shop-floor. Surely we must not try to compete with low wages in Third World countries? Surely we must aim for much better technology and higher wages?

Many of the Broadheath companies were family firms. As we have acknowledged, there is of course always a danger that successive generations of family ownership will result in complacency, inadequate investment, or just plain incompetence. Yet there was much that was good in a company in which the workpeople also were all treated as members of a family, a living community. It is surely inconceivable that in such a company, its most senior members would pay themselves huge bonuses at a time when they were sacking large numbers of their workpeople and reducing the pay of those who remained.

Some readers may be surprised that there has been little mention in this book of trade unions. Some, indeed, may even declare that most of the problems of Broadheath stemmed from the attitudes and activities of the unions. Part of the answer to such a charge might well be that, given the general disposition of the two sides of industry, reflecting the class structure of society, and the many shortcomings of managers in British industry, management got unions which were no worse than they deserved.

However, on a more factual level, the great majority of Broadheath's companies reported good labour relations with virtually no 'private' strikes until they started declaring redundancies. Some former directors of companies have made general remarks disparaging unions, their restrictive practices and their responsibility for the reputation of British industry for late deliveries. Yet the reasons given for the decline of many firms in Broadheath did not normally include union difficulties as major factors. There was, of course, no way of escaping disputes at the national level, usually about pay. In some instances, it appeared there were problems with militant regional officials who seemed to be further away from the workpeople they represented than the company management.

Since Broadheath companies went into deep decline there have been many trade union reforms under government legislation. These may well have made life easier for managers but they do not appear to have solved the problems of British industry or improved the quality of management. It seems very odd indeed that the Japanese, about as foreign a race as one can get, have not only surpassed us in technology but also in industrial management so that they have not only taken over swathes of British companies, but also demonstrated to us how to organise production processes and to manage British workers – in Britain. But too late for Broadheath!

These may be regarded as matters of opinion. What is beyond dispute is that for a hundred years the Broadheath estate was the major motor of the economy of Altrincham and district, providing interesting work for many of its citizens. Many aspects of local history flow from this fact. For instance, the building of the Oldfield Brow council estate in the inter-war period may not have made sense but for the fact that the industrial estate was just a walk away along the canal. The estate certainly raised the level of wages in the area and thus may well have contributed to the demise of the mansions of Dunham Massey as the cost of servants became prohibitive.

It seems astonishing that the loss of thousands of industrial jobs in the 1970s and 1980s did not have a more disastrous effect on local people than it did. However, Altrincham was not quite in the same category as those great industrial or mining areas which lost all hope when their major employers disappeared. Proximity to Manchester still paid dividends in terms of suburban wealth. Greater mobility in the days of spreading car ownership and wider public transport has meant that Altrincham people travel far and wide to work. The growth of Manchester Airport has brought many jobs for local people. Yet many men and women, particularly those aged over fifty, are idle.

In an earlier chapter we speculated that a significant factor leading to the closure of Churchills in 1972 was the severe reduction in the motor cycle business of BSA who were taken over by Alfred Herbert in 1967, having themselves taken over Churchills in 1961. In September 1995 the *Daily Telegraph* published the story of a sequel in the motor cycle industry. By 1973, it said, Japanese competition had forced a merger between the British producers Triumph, BSA and Norton, and a co-operative was formed. Despite substantial government help, in 1983 the liquidators were called in.

In that same year a British businessman with no manufacturing or motor cycle experience – Mr John Bloor – bought the Triumph trademark for £138,000, assembled half a dozen designers and engineers, none of them with experience of the industry and set about designing and making a British motor bike.

The project was controlled with great care, involving detailed market assessment. The only real competition was from Japan, but, increasingly, the huge industrial success of that country has brought about its own correction, i.e. a large increase in the value of the yen, making Japanese products less competitive and leading to a slump in the country in the 1990s.

So the market prospects for the new British motor cycle – the Thunderbird – seem to be very good. Making the bikes has been a lot harder. The *Telegraph* report says, "The main problem has been the inability of British industry to supply the parts through a mixture of apathy and incompetence." Mr Bloor said, "It's disgusting. When I first set up Triumph, we did not realise that manufacturing technology in Britain is extremely poor. In many cases sub-contractors were incompetent in cost-control, quality and service."

The catalogue of failure was depressing. High-technology ingredients, from instruments to carburettor, brakes to suspension, are imported, mainly from Japan. British Steel would not supply high-tensile tubular steel for the frames except on a ten-year contract; in Japan is was easy to buy the material to order. Even the con-rods have come from Germany. And so on.

In 1994-95, Triumph broke even. In 1995 it is producing 15,000 machines and is moving soon to new plant on a 40 acre site.

This story seems to be typical of British industry – strong individual initiative showing enterprise and control but conspicuous and isolated on a sea of mediocrity and incompetence. In retrospect, Broadheath seems to have been well above average in Britain but swamped by the tide of national industrial decline.

XII
EPILOGUE

What would the proverbial visitor from Mars – or even from Manchester – make of Atlantic Street on a first visit in 1995? The entry from the Manchester Road is inauspicious enough with the unlovely retail warehouse sheds and their sprawling car parks on the left, where Luke and Spencer and Richards had early plants, and the bleak, unadorned and almost anonymous production sheds of a printing company on the right where once stood proud Thornton-Pickards and later Tilghmans.

But worse is to come for the exploring visitor as there opens up the visit of a hotch-potch of higgledy-piggledy buildings, empty sites annexed by untidy car parks, apparently a cement works (!) on the right and another dust producing industrial operation on the left. The eye moves from the ancient frontages of industrial companies to more modern plain blocks of offices housing a multitude of company offices. A little street of recently removed houses appears. Then there are the vast factory premises of yesteryear, some put to multiple use by

54. Cement Works?

small commercial concerns, others boarded-up and ugly in their vacant desolation.

There is clear evidence that the main Atlantic Street has been resurfaced in recent years and lining one side for 100 yards or so there are even real trees, where Churchills playing fields have been covered with a business park. However, as one wanders down the little side streets along abominable surfaces one feels like an explorer again. Two narrow lanes duck under the railway to the vast derelict former factories of Richards and Tilghmans, part occupied by a steel distributor and part by the small remaining premises of Tilghman-Wheelabrator. Even the book distributing library has decamped. Most of this once vital machine tools site is destined to become another retail warehouse site challenging and prejudicing Altrincham town centre.

What does the intrepid new visitor make of all this? Could he perhaps, covering his eyes momentarily with a cautious hand, wonder whether he was in a perverted time warp, going back forty odd years to some defeated country, bombed half to rubble, where the survivors have individually struggled to gain a precarious living by squatting among old buildings, some more or less intact, others derelict, some long gone? Would he not then marvel at the enterprise of so many sur-

55. Vital connecting road?

vivors in the midst of the desert of absent communal organisation or effort? Yet the street has been resurfaced, so something is stirring in local government!

Further on, too, there is a new road linking the street to new business offices to the north. On the far reaches of the street itself there are sparkling new premises for smallish companies – a few moderate sized industrial concerns even. Perhaps the owners of these are the commercial representatives of a victorious occupying power, despising the old massive native industrial operations?

Yet all is not quite what it seems in the heart of the street. Look carefully and although you will see some faded old industrial names – Charles Madan, and Atlantic Rubber, for instance. P I Castings is actually operating well. Standing proud along the frontage of a large brick building is the name RECORD ELECTRICAL and next door in the original building of that company is the ATLANTIC BUSINESS CENTRE, run by Ken Cooper who was involved in the 1985 management buy-out of Record Electrical.

The noticeboard outside the business centre displays some 40 names of companies who between them occupy nearly all the former premises of Record Electrical. The Record company itself still occupies a large part of one floor making on a small scale much the same measuring instruments as it did decades ago. Mr Cooper has brought into the building several small companies from various parts of the

56. Closed down! Castleton Street can be seen beyond C S Madan. Inside is a furniture workshop. Castleton Steam Packing was in the building beyond.

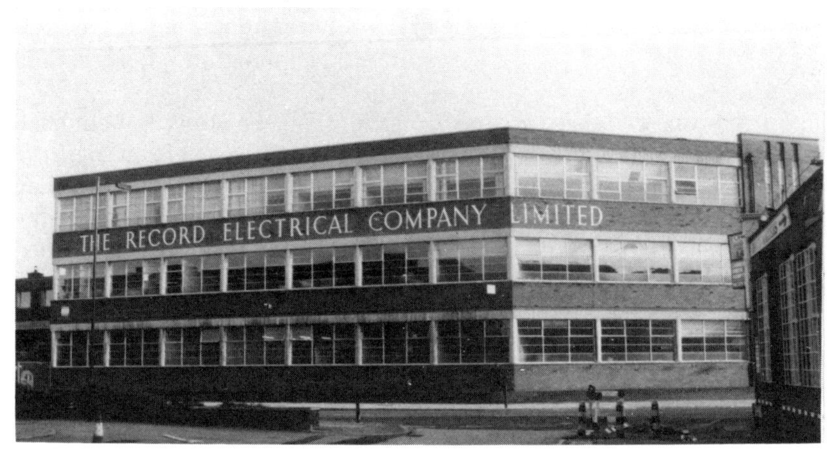

57. Record Electrical – who now occupy part of the middle floor.

country who use the Record instruments for products provided for environmental work – a kind of vertical integration.

The rest of the premises is let to a great variety of companies many of them basically offices but there is one quite old-fashioned workshop where a few craftsmen earn their living with their hands on metal work – what a wondrous miscellany of enterprise is there! There is even a friendly café-bar where one can have a light lunch with a glass of beer.

There are many small businesses too across the canal where the successors to Linotype and Budenbergs fight to keep their operations going. The vast former Linotype factory is shared with a variety of businesses and most notably with the NOVA Group, making double glazing and conservatories, taking up a great acreage of space.

So, amongst all the sad dereliction of a great industrial estate, there can be found, if the visiting explorer looks hard, much vitality in a myriad of smaller forms. "After all," he might well say, "we won the real war anyway and now we are winning the battles in the new era of small scale enterprises, some of them even making things."

Well, yes, but we have lost the main industrial battles. Making things on a large scale is still the most vital economic activity but so much of it is now undertaken elsewhere and especially overseas, and to some extent by foreign-owned companies in Britain, A few years ago our balance of payments was in record deficit, recently reduced by recession, but ever threatening to resurface as a major restraint. With a

58. Atlantic Business Centre – formerly the original Record Electrical building.

much truncated industrial base, expanding home demand leads soon to bottlenecks, inflation and increased imports.

As this book was nearing completion, *The Guardian* newspaper published a report of a banquet in the City of London when the managing director of GEC seized the opportunity to lambast the British obsession with moving money around rather than creating wealth. Commending the youngish financial operators to pick up their table napkins, write letters of resignation and come and join industry, he said that the relative decline of manufacturing over the last twenty years was a result of dreadful management, because the City was creaming off the best and brightest of Britain's youth. The director of the London University Career Service agreed that many of the best students still opt for the glamour of a City job – mainly because the pace of progress in industry is too slow. It was also recognised that manufacturing also has an image problem. So the Mansion House guests who hesitated to give up their City careers were advised —

> "Teach children that where there's brass there does not necessarily have to be muck."

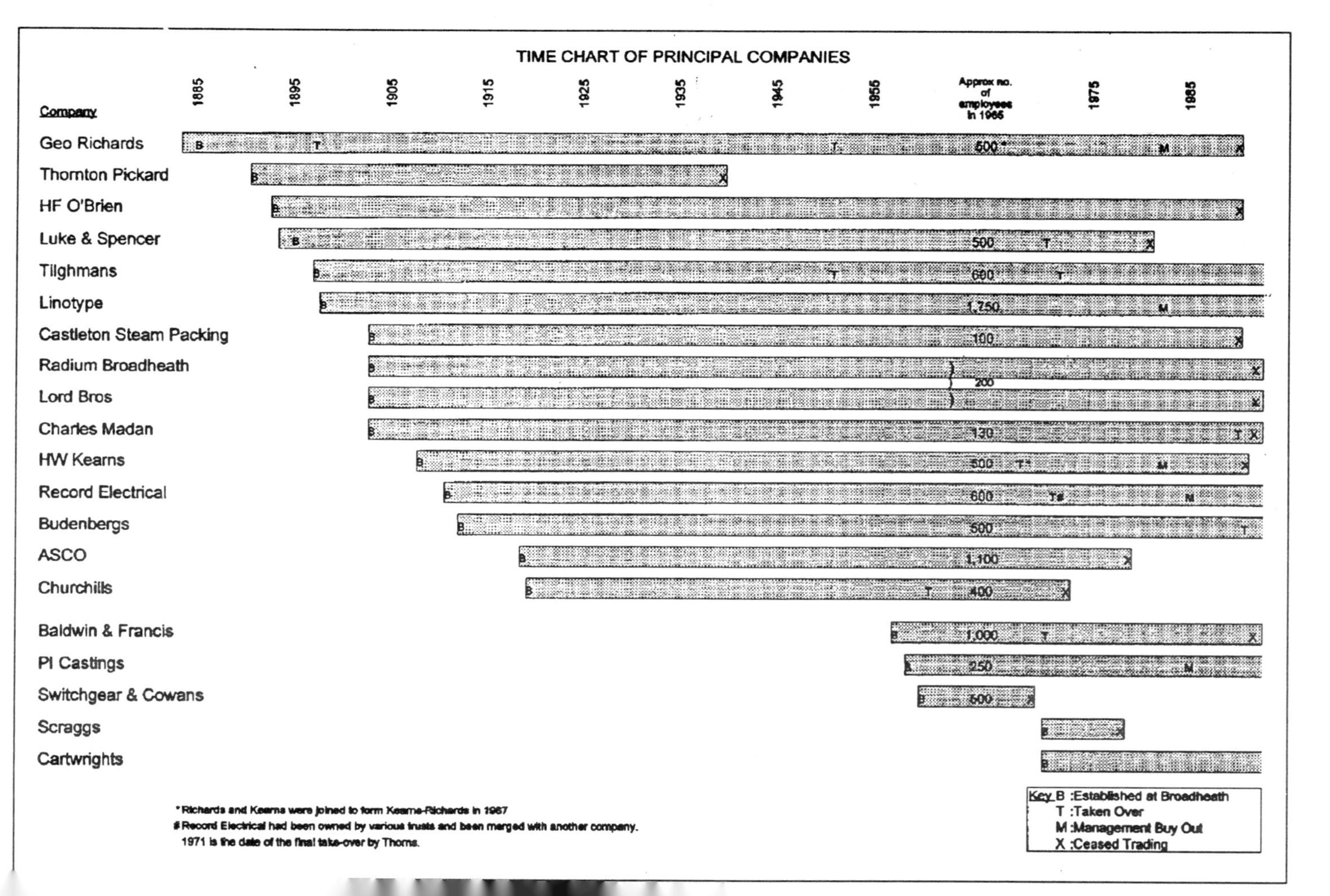

* Richards and Kearns were joined to form Kearns-Richards in 1967

Record Electrical had been owned by various trusts and been merged with another company. 1971 is the date of the final take-over by Thorns.

SOURCES AND ACKNOWLEDGEMENTS

The greater part of the information for this book has come from the files of local newspapers, particularly those of the *County Express*, published for a few years around 1960, and the *Altrincham Guardian*, all held in Trafford Local Studies Centre in Sale Library. This information has been greatly amplified by discussions with a number of past and present directors and employees of the major companies including:

Mr Ken Albutt, Managing Director of the ATR Group which includes P I Castings Ltd;
Mr Jim Bradshaw, formerly Internal Auditor, Linotype and Machinery Ltd;
Mr Brian Bottomley, formerly Technical Director of Churchills and later Managing Director of Kearns-Richards who led the management buy-out of the company;
Mr Nigel Bottomley, accountant, son of Brian, who was also involved with the buy-out;
Mr Brian Budenberg, formerly Managing Director of Budenberg Ltd;
Mr Peter Cartwright, Joint Managing Director of the Cartwright Group;
Mr Ken Cooper, Managing Director of Record Electrical Company;
Mr Graham Chapman, formerly service engineer/demonstrator, George Richards and Company Ltd;
Mr Roy Hurst, formerly machine tools inspector, George Richards and Company Ltd;
Mr John Parsons, formerly Managing Director and Chairman of Linotype and Machinery Ltd;
Mr Keith Plant, General Manager of Spares and Services of Tilghman Wheelabrator Ltd;
Mr Norman Spilisbury, formerly Works Managers of Budenberg Ltd;
Mr A H Walker, formerly Sales Director of Linotype and Machinery Ltd.

In addition to providing valuable information about their own companies – and in some cases photographs and documents – many of these gentlemen contributed important opinions and information about other companies and about Broadheath in general.

Other information and views on Broadheath companies were obtained from *Altrincham – a history,* edited by Don Bayliss, published by Willow Publishing in 1992, particularly the chapter by Dr Curtis Sparkes, formerly Technical Director and then Managing Director of H W Kearns and Company Ltd.

Reference was also made to Dr Sparkes's unpublished MSc Thesis of 1988 in UMIST Library – 'History of Horizontal Boring Machines with special reference to the Manchester Engineering Companies of Pearns, Richards and Kearns'.

Information was obtained from a number of company leaflets and brochures in Altrincham Reference Library including those published by Linotype and Machinery Ltd, Churchills and Thornton-Pickards. On the latter company reference was also made to Mr D Rendell's book *The Thornton-Pickard Story* published by himself and the Photographers' Collectors' Club of Great Britain in 1992.

Reference is made in the text to Charles Nickson's book *Bygone Altrincham,* published by Mackie and Co. Ltd, 1935, and to three books by the author of this book from which material has been drawn:

Trade for the People, published by the Book Guild Ltd in 1990
Mansions and Men of Dunham Massey, published by the author in 1991
The Making of Altrincham 1850 to 1991, published by the author in 1991

Most of the general economic information in this book is drawn from *Trade for the People* and the local information about Altrincham and district from the other two books, and the many references in those books are not repeated here.

Reference is made in the text to the important book by Will Hutton, *The State We're In,* published by Jonathan Cape in 1995

*

The author is grateful to the following people, in addition to those in the above list of people interviewed.

Hilda and Don Bayliss, respectively Secretary and Chairman of Altrincham History Society, who commented on the first draft and made important general comments. Don Bayliss also made numerous textual suggestions, many of which were adopted.

Colin Graham, history teacher, who also read and commented on the first draft and made some important suggestions.

Jill Groves of Northern Writers Advisory Services for editing and typesetting this book to her usual very high standards.

Jayne Britton, Librarian of Trafford Local Studies Centre and her colleagues for great and willing assistance in viewing microfilms and producing maps and old newspapers.

Valerie Freeman of Altrincham Library, who energetically helped me to find books, pamphlets and old maps.

R M Dodsworth, Director of Estates and Economic Development of Trafford Metropolitan Council, who lent me files relevant to Broadheath industry.

My son Colin Bamford for devoting much time and skill to taking the photographs and for commenting helpfully on the text.

*

The following illustrations have been photographed by Colin Bamford from brochures: 5, 6, 7, 10, 11, 12, 14, 15, 16, 23, 33, 35 in Altrincham Reference Library; 19, 36, 37, 38 from newspapers in Trafford Local Studies Centre. These have been reproduced with the permission of Altrincham Reference Library and Trafford Local Studies Centre. Three photographs, 24, 25 and 42, have been reproduced by permission of Brian and Nigel Bottomley. The rest have been taken by Colin Bamford and are in the author's own collection.

Index

FRANK BAMFORD

After over twenty years' experience of international business, Frank Bamford began to write books based on his experience and his long interest in economics. Firstly, he wrote *Trade for the People* relating the economic history of Britain since the Industrial Revolution. Next came two books depicting the impact of national events on the Altrincham district only ten miles from the seat of the Industrial Revolution in South Lancashire and Manchester.

Mansions and Men of Dunham Massey told the story of the unique estate of great houses built in the mid-Victorian years on the south-west flank of Altrincham with wealth from the cotton industry.

The Making of Altrincham related the economic and social history of Altrincham in the last century and a half.

Now BROADHEATH completes the local trilogy by describing the rise and fall of industry on the north-west flank of Altrincham.

Frank Bamford takes an active part in local affairs in his adopted town of Altrincham where he has lived for thirty years. As Chairman of the Civic Society he is closely concerned with the future development of the Victorian town. As Chairman of school governors and in other activities he is very much involved in the life of the town in 1995.